HOW TO CHOOSE
AND BUY AN RV

Here's how to get it right first and every time

Collyn Rivers

RVBooks.com.au (2020)

Publishing Details

Publisher: RV Books, 2 Scotts Rd, Mitchells Island, NSW, 2430. info@rvbooks.com.au

How to choose and buy an RV. Edition 1: 2020.

ISBN: 978-0-6487945-5-4

Publisher's Notes: To ensure topicality, this book is updated when necessary.

Disclaimer: Every effort has been made to ensure that the information in this book is accurate; however, no responsibility is accepted by the author or publisher for any error or omission or any loss, damage or injury suffered by anyone on the information or advice, or from any other cause.

The author would appreciate feedback relating to any errors or omissions.

Front cover photo by Nubia Navarro, Bogota, Columbia. Back cover photo by the author.

RV Books has made every effort to acknowledge the copyright of photographs in this book. Please advise any errors or omissions. We rectify as quickly as possible.

Chapter List

Chapter 1 – Establishing the essentials   1

Chapter 2 - Towed – or self-propelled?   6

Chapter 3 - RV categories   13

Chapter 35 - RV awnings and annexes   36

Chapter 5 - RV kitchens   38

Chapter 6 - RV showers and toilets and washing machines   43

Chapter 7 - Dining and sleeping   52

Chapter 8 - RV accessories   56

Chapter 9 – Buying the RV   67

Chapter 10 – Looking after yourself and your RV   78

Chapter 11 – Useful RV-related books and information   84

Chapter 12 – About the author   86

Appendix 1 – RV terminology   89

Appendix 2 – Australian Road Rules Summary   94

Appendix 3 – (New) Road Vehicles Act 2018   104

Appendix 4 – Checklist for buying a used RV   107

Appendix 5 – Australian Consumer Warranties   110

Appendix 6 – RV checking and loading   113

CHAPTER I

Establishing the essentials

An RV is a considerable investment. You need to ensure it is the right thing for you and, if applicable, for a partner. As well as seeing new places and people, RV travel can involve long distances, loneliness and frustration. It also requires teamwork and multiple tasking and can be stressful and hard work. Most people like it, some love it, but it is not for everyone.

Those likely to enjoy the RV lifestyle are likely to enjoy exploring, being outdoors, socialising and at least tolerate cooking.

Ideally, they can fix things that go wrong, and (while probably having a Plan B) do not overly worry about what happens next.

Those people probably unsuited to the RV life may have routine long-established social and family networks. They may prefer fixed routines, dislike cooking or DIY (doing it yourself) or lack affinity with nature.

Consider where you plan to go and for how long. How much you can afford to budget for purchasing and using your RV and the type of RV, i.e. camper trailer, caravan, or motorhome that suits your circumstances and your budget. You also need to consider where to store it when it is not in use. It helps talk to those already travelling; however, many tend to adapt to that which they already have.

It is essential not to create a close to a full-size kitchen on wheels: this can and does happen if either partner insists on that being conditional. Why this matters is that you're cooking and eating habits rapidly change in favour of more uncomplicated routines.

Almost all RV owners cook outside (the more experienced have an external slide-out kitchen). You are likely to use an internal kitchen only if the weather precludes cooking outside.

Figure 1.1. The author's previously-owned 1974 VW Kombi in camp near Boulia (Qld) – his wife (Maarit) is admiring the sunset. Pic: rvbooks.com.au.

Selling your home is a financial trap

Do not sell your home to finance a travelling lifestyle because RVs depreciate, whereas house prices rise. Those who sold up to buy an RV may never again be able to afford to buy a house or home unit. It is far from unknown, for those who sold an original home, to sell the RV after a year or two and buy a new home.

Rather than selling your property, consider buying a cheaper RV and have an estate agent let and manage that property. Use any rental income to fund your travelling. Other outgoing costs may be real estate agent commissions, possible furniture storage, council rates, and repairs and maintenance.

If you let your existing property, landlord insurance is essential. There are horror stories of tenants trashing properties. An alternative is to buy and, if permitted, let a property in one of the increasing numbers of communities that cater primarily for RV owners who are away in their RVs from time to time.

It is necessary to budget not just for buying the RV and your living expenses while away, but also for its ongoing maintenance, registration and insurance.

Some outgoings may be lower than when living at home, e.g. electricity, gas and water. There are fuel costs and caravan park fees if you stay in any.

You need to ensure you have an income while on the road, and whether it is enough to allow you to enjoy your travels - or merely survive.

The kind of travelling you have in mind substantially determines the type and size of RV to buy. In general, the longer your trips, the more you are likely to need creature comforts. Doing so may take up more space and require a larger RV, but one that is too large restricts where you can take it. If a caravan, the smallest you are likely to find feasible is about 4.5 metres (14 ft).

If you decide to set aside a year in your life to drive around Australia or explore its centre, then, after careful planning, do it. But also consider more but shorter trips. Doing so allows you to keep in touch with friends and family at home.

Will you be staying mainly in caravan parks or heading to remote areas? Think about this carefully since RVs tend to be designed for one purpose, or the other, but rarely both.

Assessing your probable length of stay in each place is desirable. An RV that takes an hour to set up and pull down if you are moving sites every 24 hours will likely prove tedious. Here, a campervan or motorhome may better suit. They are quicker and easier to place on-site and often fully self-contained.

RV accessibility – for those less mobile

Consider your health. Are you and your travelling companions fit enough to travel? What physical labours are involved, and can you cope with them, for example, changing a motorhome wheel and tyre that may weigh 30 kg or more?

Check how far you will be from the nearest hospital if you plan to visit remote areas. Also, check, your travel insurance covers medical treatment away from home, and even evacuations by air?

Less mobile travellers can enjoy their holidays as much as everyone else. While the RV rental market lags in providing accessible RVs, those seeking to buy one will have several from which to choose.

Accessibility features available include an accessible interior with wider doorways and handrails with everything reachable and usable when seated in a wheelchair. There are also wheelchair ramps to the RV's entrance door or wheelchair lifts.

Also valuable are remote-controlled and electric-assisted jockey wheels, stabilisers, awnings and entertainment, easily accessible beds and tables, roll-in bathrooms, and specialised storage for ramps and wheelchairs.

An RV maker may be able to modify one of their standard RVs. Doing so, however, increases weight, so discuss the implications to ensure you are within legal weight limits with ample allowance for food and personal belongings.effects.

Companies specialising in designing and building RVs for the less mobile in Australia include Accessavan (accessavan.com.au) and Problem Management Engineering and Westernport (chris@westernportcaravans.com.au).

A few RV makers have individual mobility models.

Figure 2.1: The Winnebago Forza suits people with movement issues. Several Australian companies can similarly modify RVs. Pic: Winnebago (USA).

How many people may travel in your RV?

Is it clear how many people are travelling initially? How many beds are needed, and what if circumstances change? Will children always want to go with you? What if grandchildren come along in the future? And do you have friends or relatives who may wish to travel with you?

Figure 3.1: Caravan annexe and children.
Pic: source unknown.

Accommodating more people

RV's do not have to be so large that they can cope with more people occasionally. Alternatives are to tell your friends to buy or rent an RV and travel in convoy, or to put older children in a close-by tent or annexe.

Think hard about who drives. Distances covered can be longer if there is more than one driver. If travelling with a partner, both need to be able and willing to drive. In a medical emergency, it could be essential and especially in remote areas.

CHAPTER 2

Towed – or self-propelled?

Here, you have to make a fundamental decision: 'do I want an RV that I have to tow or one that propels itself?'

One significant advantage of a towed RV is that once you have uncoupled the trailer, you can more freely explore the area in that vehicle alone.

A two-part combination also eases shopping, and even more so if you carry a small chest fridge in the tow vehicle. If staying in a caravan park, the caravan stays too, ensuring no-one else moves onto 'your' site.

A camper trailer or small caravan is towable to more places, including many a secluded riverside campsite. Beware, however, of makers' claims for 'off-road' capability. To RV makers and particularly vendors, 'off-road' can mean anything between crossing the Simpson desert – to any road lacking a white line up its centre.

Truly off-road camper-trailers exist, but only a very few caravans and the latter need a big and heavy 4WD tow vehicle (Figure 1.2).

Figure 1.2: Not for the novice RV owner – an off-road Bushtracker on tow. Pic: Bushtracker.

Camper-trailers and conventional caravans

Camper-trailers and caravans are generally cheaper to buy than motorhomes mainly because they have no engine or transmission.

There is little that wears out except tyres, shock absorbers, brake linings and wheel bearings. They are far less expensive to maintain than powered vehicles and depreciate less. Many retain their original buying price.

A towed RV needs hitching to the tow vehicle, but once you have grasped the technique, it requires little physical effort.

Conventional caravans also require a more extended, (minor) physically demanding process to set up and break-down camp, and especially to move them short distances for parking or when storing. If this is an issue, powered add-on mechanisms are readily available from caravan accessory suppliers.

It is also necessary to know about and master the interactions between tow vehicle and trailer. These include correctly matching trailer and tow vehicle, loading requirements and the likely need for stability-enhancing technology. You can readily gain this knowledge by doing a one-day caravan towing course.

Caravan safety when towed

There are next to no towing issues with camper trailers, and with caravans that weigh less than the tow vehicle. Long term statistics also show that drivers towing caravans are no more likely to have an accident than when not towing.

There is, however, a type of accident that primarily affects long conventional caravans that are heavier than the tow vehicle. They may jack-knife and possibly roll-over.

While this issue has existed since caravanning first began, its incidence escalated in 2015. In that year caravan makers increased production of twin-axle caravans weighing over two tonnes, despite in that same year, most makers of vehicles used for towing (particularly dual-cab utes), reducing their vehicles' weight (by decreasing chassis thickness from 3.5 mm to 3.0 mm).

Avoid these issues by never having a fully laden caravan exceed the weight of the fully-loaded tow vehicle. Have the required tow ball mass. This mass is usually about 10% of the caravan's loaded weight. While towing, particularly when overtaking, do not exceed 100 km/h. In many of the above respects, fifth wheel caravans are far less of an issue. Just why is explained below.

Fifth-wheel caravans

Fifth-wheel caravans are classified legally as caravans. Their on-road handling, however, is akin to that of long motorhomes. They rarely sway, but if they do, it is usually brief and does not affect the tow vehicle

They are also easy to reverse and, as shown in Figure 2.2, many can turn at a right angle.

Figure 2.2: Most fifth-wheel caravans can turn at 90 degrees. Pic: bigskyrv.com

Another bonus of a fifth wheel caravan is that its elevated front is above the tow vehicle's rear axle. This raised area provides about 1.5 metres of extra space. This space is restricted, however, to being a bed area with limited headroom. Or you can use it to store only light items – such as clothes and bedding.

A fifth-wheel caravan's downside is that it requires a dedicated tow vehicle that is not suitable for any other purpose. The tow vehicle must have a sizeable and heavy fifth-wheel tow hitch receiver (Figure 3.2) that takes time and effort to fit and remove. If that is not an issue, that the fifth-wheel format is far more stable is a strong case for buying one.

Figure 3.2: A fifth wheeler's hitch is heavy and large. Pic: Highjacker.

Campervans and motorhomes

The main benefit of campervans and motorhomes is that the engine, bed(s) and most else come in one package. They are simpler to drive, park and reverse than caravans.

There is also less need to worry if it is pouring with rain and you cannot find something you need. In a motorhome, you remain dry while looking for it, while with a caravan, if what you are seeking is in the tow vehicle, you may not.

The major disadvantage of all such vehicles is that once you have set up camp, you in effect lose your transport. Doing so is inconvenient when you need to go shopping. It is even more so if the vehicle requires significant repairs: you lose both home and ready mobility.

There used to be a reasonably clear distinction between campervans and the far larger motorhomes. Now, however, there is no clear dividing line, except for converted delivery vans.

Campervan and motorhomes are not ideal forms of daily transport when back home. There is also no way your kids are likely to accept being driven to and from school in one. Many motorhome owners thus need two motorised vehicles.

Motorhomes are more expensive than most camper-trailers and caravans, and significantly so compared to European prices. They also depreciate far more than do camper trailers and caravans.

Comfort is a further consideration. Generally, vehicles used for towing are quieter and more comfortable than motorhomes. Many 4WD tow vehicles have car-like suspensions, car seats and an extensive array of comfort accessories. Most motorhomes, however, have truck-based suspension and seats designed for short-haul delivery drivers, rather than long-distance travellers.

Motorhomes can also be noisy if poorly insulated or if items are not adequately secured. In contrast, with a caravan, you never hear the 'clickety-clack' of your pots and pans bouncing around in a drawer. Campervans are based on commercial delivery vans and may have similar shortcomings.

Travelling patterns

The travel patterns of caravan and motorhome owners are often different. Caravan owners tend to base their trailer at the 'hub' of an imaginary wheel and explore the 'spokes' of the local area using their tow vehicle.

Motorhome owners tend to be more nomadic: they typically travel around the 'rim' of the wheel or exploring between rim and hub, making shorter but more overnight stops.

Easing the buying decision

Various ways exist to overcome the disadvantages of each type of RV. Caravan component suppliers have many add-on devices to make towing more relaxed and safer. These include reversing cameras, stability control devices and re-mote-controlled motorised caravan movers for moving the caravan over short distances.

Weight distributing hitches transfer the effect of some of a caravan's weight from the rear axle onto the front axle of the tow vehicle but may introduce rarely realised and unde-sirable side effects (rvb.chaos-central.com/Towing-Without-a-Weight-Distributing-Hitch).

To make towing safer, buy a caravan that, when fully laden, is lighter than the fully loaded tow vehicle. Ideally, it should be less. Also, complete a caravan towing course.

Many motorhome owners have ways of increasing mobility once in camp. These range from bicycles (both pedal and powered) to motorcycles to towing a small car or even to have a small under-bed garage at their side or rear (Figure 4.2).

Figure 4.2: Volkner Mobil Performance's RV garages a small car. Pic: VMP.

If you correctly store or pull these items while driving, and do not make the RV overweight, they increase freedom.

Who buys what – and why?

There seem to be no logical reasons for choosing a caravan vs. a motorhome. A (2018) Erwin Hymer group survey that the British (72%), Dutch (56%) and Swedish (53%) prefer caravans.

Italians (at 83%) far prefer a campervan or motorhome, but most hire one - only 15% own one.

For decades, 90% of all registered RV's have been camper trailers or caravans: mostly caravans. This choice is possibly due to Australian roads being straighter and less hilly than many other countries. Furthermore, the long distances that need to be covered, even when exploring at your destination, make a separate tow vehicle handy.

You do not have to follow the crowd. The workarounds suggested above, combined with ever-changing technology, make it likely that you can use either a caravan or a motorhome successfully in most circumstances.

CHAPTER 3

RV categories

There are many different types of RVs.

Teardrop campers are compact, tear-shaped 'beds on wheels' with an outdoor rear kitchen under a raisable flap. They are small, narrow and light (weighing as little as 350 kg), and easy to tow even by motor tricycles. Storage and headroom, however, is limited.

These campers originated as (American) magazine projects for home building. The first known mention was in an article 'Modern Gypsies' in the April 1936 issue of Popular Science Monthly.

There are some beautiful examples of heritage wooden teardrops still on the road today, as well as many recently made.

Figure 1.3: Teardrop camper on-site.
Pic: Source unknown.

A Teardrop Camper magazine exists to this day: it is called Teardrops and Tiny Campers (www.cooltears.com).

The popularity of the teardrop trailer started to dwindle in the USA in the late 1950s because Americans wanted campers that were bigger and better.

Teardrop campers remained popular in Australia but threatened when the then major manufacturer, Gidget Retro Teardrop Campers, went into voluntary administration in 2019. This matter resulted in some 80 customers across Australia and America losing A$3.5 million in unreturned deposits.

Early Teardrop campers are still in use in Australia, but coffee vendors and others modify them. Several local manufacturers are once again producing traditional-looking Teardrops.

The Freemantle-based Cool Beans Campers (Figure 2.3) are virtually a replica of the original concept - complete with exposed wheels and mudguards. The roof and mudguards are of polished aluminium.

Figure 2.3. The Cool Bean Camper.
Pic: Cool Bean Campers.

Another retro-style Teardrop is Suncamper's 2.8 metre by 1.7-metre wide Smidge (Figure 3.3). Depending on options it's Tare mass (empty weight) is about 580 kg, and can carry up to 420 kg.

Figure 3.3. The Suncamper Smidge. Pic: Suncamper.

Roadstar Caravans, a company better known for top-quality full-size products, builds a slightly larger Teardrop-shaped unit (Figure 4.3). It is a top-of-the-range product that uses fibreglass sandwich panel construction. It has a tare weight of 590 kg and can carry up to 300 kg.

Figure 4.3. The Roadstar Colt product.

Figure 5.3. The Riptide Breeze camper.
Pic: RipTide Campers.

At 4.45 metres long, 2.02 metres wide and 1.84 metres high, the Riptide Breeze (Figure 5.3) is slightly larger than most. Its Tare weight is 780 kg, and it can carry 120 kg payload.

The maker says it provides about 30% more interior space and more usable storage.

Tent trailers

People seeking a marginally-less uncomfortable form of tent camping often buy basic tent trailers. The tent folds out from a box trailer base, usually with the bed within that trailer. There is either a fold-out or slide-out kitchen. Most are relatively light, so can be towed by a wide range of vehicles and are rugged enough to travel wherever the tow vehicle can go.

While cheap and straightforward, these trailers may take a long time to set-up and then pack up and have limited storage capacity when closed.

Tent trailers' canvas weather protection renders them challenging to pack up in (or after) wet weather or dew. If not correctly cared for, that canvas may leak or cause odours over time.

Basic camper-trailers

Basic camper-trailers are marginally more elaborate tent trailers. They typically have a (slide-out) kitchen, storage lockers, battery, fridge (or fridge compartment), lighting and a comfortable bed enclosed in canvas. They cost more than tent trailers, but are more comfortable.

Some camper-trailers may have a fold-down section, which provides a solid internal floor. Basic camper-trailers are more flexible than tent trailers. They have the same disadvantages of tent trailers in the canvas department. New tent materials to replace canvas are now available. Such materials may, to some extent, mitigate the problems.

There are now many imported camper-trailers. Care needs to be taken when buying as quality varies from dreadful to excellent. There are, however, many local makers.

Up-market camper-trailers

These more complex and costly type of camper-trailers now form a small but growing sector of the market. These camper-trailers have far less, or no canvas - achieved by having rigid sides and roofs made of fibreglass, sandwich panels, powder-coated steel or powder-coated aluminium.

*Figure 6.3. The 2019 TVan Mk 5. This truly go-anywhere Australian-designed and built camper trailer is thoroughly tried and tested.
Pic: Track Trailer.*

Slide-out external kitchens and even an en-suite toilet and shower may be included, along with a fridge, lighting and some (often optional) hot water and heating. Some withstand severe off-road use.

Pop-top caravans

These units have a roof that lowers for towing and is raised while on-site. Their low profile reduces wind drag, but their lifting roofs can be heavy and hard to open unless fitted (as some are) by sprung or winch lifting mechanisms. Nor can they have the peripheral overhead lockers provided with many caravans.

They are reasonably priced and lightweight, but most have only essential facilities. For reasons unclear, pop-tops tend to appeal to first-time caravan buyers.

Full height single-axle caravans

Full height single-axle caravans are limited by generally available tyre size to about two tonnes and in Australia are rarely longer than five metres.

These caravans can be of many shapes, sizes and construction materials. As typical with most caravans, they are wider than camper-trailers and their towing vehicles, enabling them to offer more facilities.

The European-made versions are generally 30% t0 40% lighter (per metre) than Australian made caravans (and some are longer). The difference is, however, narrowing as Australian makers increasingly adopt European caravan body construction techniques. Prices vary according to size, facilities and materials used.

Full height dual-axle caravans

Most full height dual-axle caravans have generous accommodation including island beds, dedicated dining-areas fair-sized kitchens, and often separate toilets and showers.

Some dual axle caravans weigh over three tonnes. Only a very few 4WD tow vehicles are capable of towing these massive caravans safely.

Toy hauliers

A toy haulier is a large box trailer that doubles as a garage on wheels. The 'toys' are generally for adults and include bicycles, motorcycles, quad-bikes and even small boats.

Frontal accommodation enables owners to have their toys with them on the road. Toy hauliers can be as plush as expensive traditional caravans. Note: when seeking further information, many local vendors use the American spelling 'toy haulers'.

Figure 7.3: New Age XU toy haulier.
Pic: caravancampingsales.com.au

The 6.7 metres (22ft) XU shown in Figure 7.3 is multi-purpose. It is usable for family holidays, a mobile office or event HQ. It can sleep up to eight, depending on configuration, as long as the toys are parked outside.

Always load toy haulers following manufacturers' recommendations. The weight and (particularly location) of heavy items within such towed trailers significantly affects their on-road stability.

Off-road caravans

As with camper trailers, there is no legal definition of an off-road caravan: it is whatever its maker or vendor wants it to be. In broad terms, it should have improved body protection, raised and well-damped suspension and a more robust chassis that is cutaway at the rear. Such features enable that caravan to be towed on poor quality dirt roads and even across shallow rivers with reduced risk of damage.

Figure 8.3. This Trakmaster 3.9 metre (13 ft) Australian designed and made caravan is one of the very few genuinely off-road units. Pic: Trakmaster.

While their weight is counterproductive for towing off-road, most such caravans are much heavier than their 'on-road' counterparts. They may also have bigger water tanks and a more extensive range of 12-volt appliances for bush camping. Some are so massive they need a light truck to pull them.

Many people buy off-road caravans because they are often more sturdily made. Such caravans are expensive. They are rarely if ever, taken off-road. The caravan parks in Alice Springs have many such caravans while their owners explore off-road in their 4WD tow vehicles.

Fifth-wheel caravans

The term 'fifth-wheel' stems from the flat plate coupling used on commercial semi-trailers. The trailer's pivoting mechanism is directly above the rear axle of the tow vehicle rather than behind it. This hitch placing enables fifth-wheel caravans to imposes no side 'yaw' forces on the tow vehicle. Fifth-wheel caravans are far more stable than any conventional caravan. Towing one is not unlike driving a long coach.

Because the tow vehicle carries far more of its weight, a fifth-wheel caravan can support a much higher load than can a conventional caravan. Furthermore, because its raised front section overlaps the tow vehicle, that section adds a metre or more usable space. That extra space, however, is confined to use for sleeping or storage as it has only a metre or so headroom.

Figure 9.3: The Queensland (Australia) built Winjana RV Cattai. Pic: caravancampingsales.com.au.

The fifth-wheel caravan's main downside is that a specialised tow vehicle is required, and is not readily usable for other use. A significant plus is that a fifth-wheeler has excellent on-road stability.

Fixed roof campervans

Fixed roof campervans are many young people's entry to independent travelling. Beds have to be made up each night (if the occupants are not sleeping on the beach). Cooking facilities are limited, and their owners generally use public washing and toilet facilities.

The iconic Volkswagen Kombi is the best-known example. Based on the VW Transporter van platform, these campervans have been produced since the 1950s and provide simple, cheap accommodation on the road.

While it has been out of production for some years, the Kombi-style California Beach locked in for a launch in the third quarter of 2020. A new engine and transmission combination also becomes available. It is a 110kW/340Nm turbo-diesel unit paired to a dual-clutch automatic and Volkswagen's 4Motion all-wheel-drive system.

As well as a few big manufacturers' conversions, many private companies convert delivery vans into a range of fixed roof campervans - from bare essentials - to high end.

Pop-top campervans

A pop-top roof increases headroom by including a PVC extension. The raisable roof also improves ventilation and increased natural light.

Particularly for tall people, pop-top camper vans are a more liveable proposition than their fixed-roof counterparts. New models are now offering a bed that drops down from the roof. VW is the international leader in this sector, but Mercedes has joined this sector with its new Marco Polo.

Slide-on unit campervans

Slide-on campervans are similar to hybrid camper-trailers but with the removable (slide-on) accommodation held over the vehicle rather than towed behind it. Some older slide-on units were detachable. Most slide-on units these days remain more or less bolted permanently in place.

*Figure 10.3: Slide-on camper Earthcruiser Express.
Pic: Earthcruiser Express.*

A range of vehicles can be modified to accept a slide-on. Care must be taken not to exceed the vehicle's maximum permitted weight.

Some are so massive that there is minimal weight allowance for personal effects. The one shown in Figure 10.3, however, is relatively light (at a stated 280 kg).

Utility conversions (utes)

When converted to RV form, trade-peoples' utility vehicles (known invariably in Australia as 'utes') often have an area built over the driving cab as well as the tray. Doing so provides a more extensive living and sleeping area while containing overall length to that of the basic unit.

The Toyota Hilux and the Ford Explorer are the most common utes converted to campers. Such conversions are appealing because they can be driven and parked in much the same way as a standard ute with no towing issues, yet having adequate facilities. Four-wheel-drive versions are also available.

Figure 11.3: Care is needed not to overload these conversions: they can and do bend, particularly if end-heavy: Pic: Whichcar.com.au

Delivery van conversions

Delivery van conversions are a compromise between campervans and full-sized motorhomes. They can be a cost-effective option for buyers since most conversion companies work within the existing van body framework, reducing structural changes to a minimum.

The most popular such conversions are of Fiat Ducato and Mercedes Sprinter vans. Most are available in lengths of six to seven metres, a choice of engine sizes and suspension options. Facilities can be extensive and often include a toilet and shower.

These conversions are popular with motorhome rental companies. Buyers of such vehicles need to be aware that, unless modified, motor engineers design the suspension to carry goods – not people.

On the plus side, slide-out beds and kitchens are now available with vehicles at the top end of this market.

Low profile campervans and motorhomes

Makers of some of the coach-built campervans and smaller motorhomes use only the cab, engine, gearbox and front chassis of the larger vans. That section attaches to a (typically AL-KO) rear chassis made for that purpose, and a custom-made coach section added above and to the rear of the cab. The makers import the base vehicles as back-to-back pairs (Figure 12.3).

Figure 12.3: Here's how a many a campervan begins.
Pic: Source unknown.

Without the dimensional limitations of delivery vans, these conversions are generally longer and broader, with good heat and sound insulation and well-equipped. Low profile versions have less wind drag. Because of this, they use less fuel. That low profile, however, reduces space above the cab for storage, or an extra bed.

Low profile RVs offer space, facilities and fuel economy at a reasonable cost. Typical lengths vary from 5 to 8 metres.

Seven metres is the maximum-length vehicle that can be parked unrestricted on many suburban streets.

High profile campervans and motorhomes

High profile campervans and motorhomes are much the same sizes as low profile units except for a bulbous compartment above the cab. Traditionally called a 'Luton peak' (Figure 13.3), this area is used for sleeping and storage with the bed usually accessible only by ladder.

The Luton peak concept (Figure 13.3) makes high profile campervans and motorhomes ideal for families. The overhead front end bed enables sleeping children to be away from adults.

Do not carry anything other than the mattress and bedding in the Luton peak while driving. The base vehicle is not designed or intended to be laden in this area.

Figure 13.3: Luton peak motorhome.
Pic: KEA NZ.

Due to their flexible sleeping and dining arrangements, these vehicles are also popular with hire companies. The air drag of the overhead compartment, however, increases fuel usage and reduces light entering the cabin. They tend to be less favoured by travelling couples.

A-class motorhomes

A-Class motorhome builders use the chassis and engine of a truck or coach and build everything else, including the cab. Such motorhomes have a panoramic windscreen, separate living, dining and sleeping sections. Most are long, heavy and costly.

Initially made famous by Winnebago in the USA, these motorhomes are virtually small luxury houses on wheels. They consume a lot more fuel than most other RVs and can be challenging to manoeuver due to their width and length.

Figure 14.3. The A-class Jayco Adelaide. Pic: Jayco.

Coach conversions

Coach converters take a (usually) second-hand coach or bus, rip out the seats and convert that remaining into a motorhome.

The Toyota Coaster (Figure 14.3) is the most usual choice due to its legendary reliability, longevity and ease of conversion.

Figure 15.3: The long-wheelbase version of the Toyota Coaster is often the basis for DIY conversions. Pic: Australian Motorhomes.

Many such coaches are Japanese imports where their legal usage as a coach is limited to three years. They may have several hundred thousand kilometres on the clock. Such usage as long-distance driving causes far less wear than shorter but more frequent driving.

Figure 16.3: The 7 metre Hino coach is also becoming popular for DIY conversions. Pic: K. Allen.

A few niche businesses supply parts for these do-it-yourself projects. There are also many partly converted such coaches offered for sale on the used RV market. See 'Self-Built RVs' below.

'Off-road' motorhomes

A small section of the motorhome market is 'off-road' motorhomes. Users include miners, overland travel companies and intrepid explorers. These vehicles are all four- or six-wheel driven.

They go just about anywhere and are almost indestructible. Most are uncomfortable and cumbersome, and the larger ones consume a great deal of fuel.

An OKA is a largish Australian-made example. While the vehicle was intended mainly for mining companies, it proved ideal for outback tour operators and converting to 'fully off-road' motorhomes.

Figure 17.3. The author's previously-owned OKA shown crossing the Wenlock River in northern Queensland. Pic: Maarit Rivers.

Early versions had minor suspension problems, but once fixed, an OKA has virtually legendary reliability. One, owned by the author, crossed Australia via dirt tracks for much of the way from Broome to Sydney and back (some 14,000 km return) over twelve times without a single break-down. Any good OKA now sells for way over twice its new price.

The most popular similar such vehicles today are equally reliable but have a much harsher ride. Those most commonly used are based on Iveco chassis. The Mercedes Unimog is a more costly choice and is very complex mechanically.

Expedition vehicles

Those experienced in travelling remote parts of the world agree that the maximum recommended vehicle weight is about five tonnes. This weight is also the realistic limitation of older light timber bridges that were typically rated at seven tonnes when new.

Ideally, such vehicles should be compact enough to fit into a shipping container.

The vehicle shown in Figure 18.3 is a 1940 QLR Bedford. It was built as an RAF mobile airfield control unit and had a coach-built body.

Figure 18.3: Typical bridge crossing in central Africa. This one shows the QLR Bedford in the (then) Belgian Congo. At the time this was central Africa's only north-south track. Pic: Collyn Rivers.

During 1959-1960 the author and his colleague (Tony Fleming) drove it twice across Africa via the Sahara. Apart from needing the cylinder head's valve seatings being reground a few times by ourselves, it proved 100% reliable.

That vehicle is about the maximum size and weight for such trips. Depending mainly on its remaining fuel (it held over 1000 litres) and water (400 litres), it weighed five to six tonnes and was two metres wide and seven metres long.

An excellent 43-minute video of this trip is at youtu.be/Pt-G6niRiRXk

Extreme examples of 'expedition vehicles' utilise the massive MAN eight-wheel drive chassis. Some weigh over 25 tonnes.

It is hard to take vehicles of this size seriously. They are far too heavy to cross many timber bridges in third-world countries as in Figure 18.3 above.

Some are so huge that they are suited mainly to desert crossings. There are also significant personal risks in taking vehicles costing a million dollars or more into remote areas.

These vehicles are also intended, in a heavily armoured form, for the so-called 'Armageddon' market in the USA.

Figure 19.3: Typical MAN 'expedition vehicle'.
Pic: Source unknown.

Vintage and restored RVs

There is a small but passionate group of people in Australia and New Zealand who buy old vans and convert them to retro-RVs, complete with many modern conveniences. Some companies and individuals restore vintage RVs to their 'original' condition.

The VW Kombi is the classic restoration campervan. Many restorers finish these vehicles to such high standards that they command prices well over their modern equivalent. Contact Kombiclub Australia (www.kombiclub.com) for more information.

Figure 20.3: The author restored this 1974 Wesfaila VW in 1994. It was one of the earliest RVs known to use solar. In the foreground is the author's wife – Maarit. Pic: Collyn Rivers.

For owners and budding restorers of Australian vintage caravans, there is an outstanding resource of historical information and knowledge on the Vintage Caravans forum, Vintagecaravans.proboards.com. Anything built in Australia before 1970 is almost sure to be known and discussed on this site's forum. Those embarking on a caravan restoration are also supported.

Companies who restore or assist in the restoration of older RVs in Australia include The Goodwins and Son, who convert motorhomes from scratch or modify existing motorhomes, motorhomesforyou.com.au.

Advice, plans and installations for modern van conversions are offered by Van Life Conversions vanlife.com.au and Achtung Camper achtungcamper.com.au.

Self-built RVs

Some dedicated 'DIY-ers'self-build camper-trailers and caravans in their home workshops. A great deal of spare time, patience, a well-equipped workshop, and many specialised skills are needed to complete a self-built RV. Attempt this only if you have all of these. Above all, gain prior experience for what you have in mind. Take this seriously as many self-builders sell their creation shortly after completion and start all over again.

That self-building can be successful, however, is exemplified by the extraordinary unit shown in Figure 21.3. It is an off-road conversion based on a brand new Nissan Navara ute chassis – with its original tray discarded.

Figure 21.3: Dixie (see main text).
Pic: Dick Clarke of Envirotecture (Sydney)

Dick Clarke used carbon-fibre technology. Doing so enabled its finished body shell and all fittings to weigh under 375 kg.

Dixie has an empty weight of 2380 kg and a legal payload of 420 kg. To put that into perspective, when fully laden,

Dixie weighs less than an empty LandCruiser.

Few of us have Clarke's technical knowledge and skills. If you are starting an RV project, read this wise advice from Barry Davidson, a highly experienced caravan maker and founded Caboolture Caravan Repair.

'Each year we still supply materials, advice and eventual certifications to up to a dozen or so do it yourself van builders and probably twice as many bus modifiers. I have seen some excellent jobs and also some pretty awful and costly disasters.

'Some of our clients manage to finish their project; many don't. The complexities often beat them, most often because they are hard to convince to properly plan out their method of attack before they start, and stick to the plan. Those that do find that the job flows reasonably well, particularly if they have a little more than basic hand skills.

'The bus converters are more often able to finish their projects because they do not have to worry about complexities of chassis design and bodywork. Their main problems are gas and 230-volt legality and compliance with a couple of straightforward Australian Design Rules, which are much fewer than building a caravan.

'The critical thing to remember is that, generally, it takes about three times longer than you allow for and costs at least twice as much. It is the intangibles that take the time and the additional cost. – That is little fiddly bits and hidden things that you don't see on the finished product and the timing as to when you need to do things. Miss something vital, and you may have to disassemble and start again.

If you have plenty of time and energy, it can be fun. Many triers fall by the wayside. They either leave it up to the professionals to complete or abandon the project.'

Online resources for self-builders

There are some online resources to assist those wishing to self-build, including DIY camper (diycamperconversion.com/contact) for those looking to build a camper trailer, and DIY Caravans (www.diycaravans.com.au/contact-us) for self-builders looking for RV components. There are also many YouTube videos on the subject of DIY RVs.

CHAPTER 4

RV awnings and annexes

An awning is essentially a roll out roof that you can use easily and quickly. It is great to have even if only to provide an hour or two shade (or weather protection) during a lunchtime break. It is particularly valuable for providing such sun protection in outback areas where the nearest tree maybe 100 km away.

An annexe (Figure 1.4) is an awning that also has walls and a door. The weather-resistant versions can double the RVs private space.

An enclosable annexe is particularly useful for RV owners travelling with young children and even enables you to have a smaller RV at less overall cost and weight.

Figure 1.4: An RV annexe can provide extensive living and playing space – ideal if travelling with children – but takes a fair time to erect. Pic: Source unknown

Annexes are available in any number of shapes and sizes. A custom-made annexe will cost only a little more. It enables you to specify the number, size and position of windows and doors. It is readily possible to add rooms or even en-suites extending beyond the awning. Flared annexe walls provide more floor space and assist with rainwater run-off.

Before ordering check that your RV's side windows, when opened, do not clash with the RVs extended awning arms or annexes.

Related Australian Standards define cross-flow ventilation relating to combustible gasses. You cannot have walls for your awning or annexe if you have a door, fridge or range hood venting into that part of the van. Most RV makers are aware of this. They usually locate all such appliances on the non-door side of the RV. Check this before buying.

Annexe materials

Annexes may be of vinyl, canvas or shade-cloth. Vinyl is light but prone to condensation and also traps heat.

Canvas breathes slightly but is more cumbersome. It also takes a long time to dry and must be kept dry when stored. The latest polyester material, however, dries in a few minutes.

One option is to have the top two-thirds canvas and the bottom-third vinyl. Another is to have shade-cloth annexe walls. The latter is a good compromise between keeping out rain, reasonable sun protection, but compromises privacy. It does, however, allow a breeze to flow, so there is no need for windows unless you seek side views.

When and how to use an annexe

Before using the annexe, consider the weather, your duration of stay and time of year. An annex may keep you warm outside in winter, but block winter sun. Use strong pegs, a good hammer and reflective guy ropes to secure your annex. If rain or dew is forecast on the last day of a trip, take it down and store it while it is still dry.

Most awnings only need guy ropes and pegs when there is a strong wind. Annexes, however, require many guy ropes and pegs, so take longer to take up and down. Some owners colour the tops of pegs to ease seeing them when departing.

Awning mats

Use only fine mesh awning mats that allow dirt to drop through. They also allow sunlight and water to filter through to the grass (if any). These are the only type of floor mat permitted in some National Parks. Tarpaulins are generally not allowed as ground covers as they tend to kill the grass.

An excellent form is a green mesh sold by the metre by Bunnings, Mitre Ten and similar stores. It only lasts for one season or so but is ultra-cheap and very light and compact when rolled up or folded.

CHAPTER 5

RV kitchens

Apart from the massive RVs in the USA, and converted full-size coaches, RVs have limited space and need designing accordingly. It is vital not to attempt to recreate what you have at home, and that particularly applies to kitchens.

Kitchen size and location

Most first-time owners find that their lifestyle rapidly becomes simpler than when at home. They spend far more time outdoors or in the annexe, and many make do with less paraphernalia once they know what not to take next time.

Despite the above, for both powered and towed vehicles, the kitchen and its contents are the heaviest part of an RV's living area.

For optimum towing stability, caravans need the kitchen to be centrally over the caravan's axle(s). If only a rear-end kitchen seems possible, keep it small, and ideally made of a very lightweight material such as powder-coated aluminium.

Campervans are usually extended chassis versions of converted delivery vans (often with higher roofs). A campervan's width, however, is generally limited, so its kitchen is small and along only one side. Having an external slide-out or portable LP gas cooker overcomes such space limitation.

Figure 1.5: Kitchen in Jayco Eagle (pop-top) camper.

Coach-built motorhomes and the larger caravans are broader and lengthier than campervans, thus having space for a larger kitchen (Figure 2.5).

Figure 2.5: This kitchen is in a (2018) Avida Sapphire caravan. Pic: Avida.

No need for an oven

Almost RV makers include an oven - as first-time buyers assume it to be essential. In practice, however, that oven is rarely used, not least as it makes an RV's interior uncomfortably hot. After a week or three, that oven becomes storage.

That which many RV owners set up (or install) is a fold-down or slide-out cooktop, plus preparation area, and an external water tap. They also buy a large cast-iron hotpot, or a so-called Bedourie oven - in effect a lightweight hotpot. They dig a hole and cover it with hot ashes. If doing so, always mark that smoking area to avoid walking on it with bare feet. Always make 100% sure that you extinguish a campfire before leaving the campsite.

Figure 3.5: Typical kitchen. Pic: Kimberley Kamper.

Almost all camper-trailers have an outside slide-out kitchen (Figure 3.5), and they are often optional for caravans and motorhomes. If offered, it is well worth having one.

LP gas cookers

Worldwide, LP gas is increasingly used as it causing far-lower harmful emissions than coal, charcoal or timber. It is, however, far from ideal.

Most LPG stove-tops are about 55% efficient. Newer designs include obliquely oriented ports that cause the gas to 'swirl' just before igniting. Also, rather than the traditional 'flower' gas burners, by having vertical flame burners, less heat escapes into the surrounding air. The result can be 90% fuel efficiency, but such stoves are currently so costly it might take a lifetime to break even.

Keep an eye on the colour of the flame. If it turns yellow or orange rather than blue (indicating it's not getting as hot as it should be) your cooktop isn't operating efficiently – Figure 4.5.

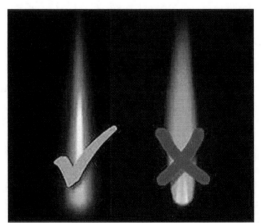

Figure 4.5: An ignited flame must be blue. If even slightly orange or red, the appliance is faulty and producing dangerous carbon monoxide. If so, have the gas system checked by a gas fitter.
Pic: Elgas.

LPG stoves heat up quickly, and temperature can be precisely controlled. Keep the flame as low as possible. Sometimes a pan may need to be open for liquids that need reducing. But where possible keep lids tightly on to trap the heat, allowing you to keep the flame lower.

Ensuring you use the right sized pot or pan for the burner also cuts your energy consumption - placing a small to pan on a large burner can waste close half of the heat.

Diesel-fuelled cooktops

Recently developed diesel-fuelled cooktops use a form of internal burning combustion that heats the cooktop's ceramic surface. There are no visible flames that might ignite a fire. Because all combustion gasses are pumped to the outside, there is no smell of diesel oil.

There are currently two leading brands: Webasto, and the Finnish-made Wallas XC Duo. When the latter unit is not in use as a cooker, it can close up to form a 1.9 kW space heater.

Most diesel units have two areas – one being the primary cooking function that is directly above the burner and a second area used for simmering. They typically use 0.09 – 0.19 litres/hour.

They take about 15 to 20 minutes to bring one litre of cold water to boiling point and about five minutes to shut down and almost an hour to cool completely. While that delay may not be acceptable in everyday domestic life, it is of less concern while camping. As long as you use good-quality substantial base cookware, their performance is otherwise similar to a household electric ceramic cooktop. The units are simple and easy to install, and anyone can legally do so. They do not need certification nor annual inspection.

Wallas also makes a diesel-fuelled oven intended market for this is marine. The unit is made to such standards and costs $5000-$10,000.

Using diesel for cooking makes sense in remote areas. Diesel, however, costs more than LP gas.

Sinks

Most RVs have a small sink, but it is often too small to be of use for washing. Many owners use a plastic bucket outside.

It's vital for RVs generally to have practical cupboards and drawers that absolutely must not self-open while driving. If necessary, add positive locks that require pushing a button.

CHAPTER 6

RV showers and toilets

Whether or not to have a shower and toilet in a small RV is related to user age and mobility, and also to the type of RV usage.

Uses who spend most nights in caravan parks may do without a shower or toilet. As with many owners of small RVs, they carry a portable toilet and use it in a small tent. By and large, however, it is feasible to include a compact shower and toilet in a 4 metre (approx. 13 ft) two-berth RV – or even smaller (Figure 1.6).

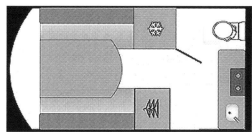

Figure 1.6: This UK-built Microlight caravan has a toilet and shower in a caravan that's body length is only 2.82 metres (9 ft). Pic: Microlight.

Portable showers and toilets

Camper-trailers and small campervans rarely have space for an en-suite. Instead, they have a portable toilet and shower in a dedicated area of an annex, or one of the small tents made for this purpose (Figure 2.6). Caravan parts suppliers sell tents made for this purpose.

As far as RV Books knows no commercially-available portable shower is acceptable for self-containment because such showers do not contain the greywater.

This restriction precludes using, for example, the CMCA's (Campervan and Motorhome Club of Australia) and some councils' RV parks that have full self-containment as a condition of usage (that includes no discharge of water). Some people, however, are experimenting with outdoor showers that trap such water.

Figure 2.6: Many owners of small RVs carry a dual toilet and shower tent such as the Weissen unit shown here. Pic: Weissen.

Larger RVs usually have an en-suite toilet, shower and washbasin. Most also have a storage cupboard, towel rails, a mirror, lighting and a combined vent and extractor fan. A few have toilets that retract under the sink or have sinks that fold up against a wall.

It assists to have more than one drainage point in the shower to ensure drainage when the van is not level, particularly with a combined shower/toilet. Also worth having are duckboards or similar means of enabling your feet to dry – especially in an en-suite area.

RV – basic toilet types

RV toilets are available in any number of models, shapes and sizes. Some, totally portable, are smaller and lower than domestic units and often made of plastic. Supporting them on a wooden base makes usage less uncomfortable – especially for tall people. The more sophisticated are generally similar to domestic toilets.

The smaller and simpler RV toilets have a cassette containing two chambers. The upper chamber has a 15-20 litre tank for flushing. The lower chamber holds liquid and solid toilet waste (plus used toilet paper) and also water and chemicals that break down the waste and destroy harmful bacteria. The more basic units have a hand pump to assist flushing. Less basic units have electric pumps.

Built-in toilets are usually larger and more substantial, and some have ceramic bowls. Other and more sophisticated toilets are described later in this chapter.

Avoid using strong domestic toilet cleaning chemicals or bleach on plastic toilets. These can harm the bowl and seat, as well as the seal between upper and lower chambers.

Toilet chemicals are needed

Human solid waste matter contains bacteria, that while beneficial within one's own body, is pathogenic to humans. Disposing of such waste matter requires adding chemicals. There are currently two major such approaches: bio-stimulant and biocides.

Bio-stimulant toilet chemicals

Bio-stimulant products are environmentally friendly. They speed up nature's otherwise aerobic breakup of faecal matter by introducing oxidising agents or enzymes. They also reduce smells. You can dispose of stimulant treated waste safely in septic, environmental or city-type sewage disposal systems.

Biciodic toilet chemicals

A biocide approach destroys life by poisoning. It is environmentally undesirable, particularly for disposal in septic tanks, in that it kills all bacteria: both wanted and unwanted. A liquid so treated is allergenic. Some people claim it is possibly also carcinogenic. It requires a heavy chemical to reduce the stench of the hydrogen sulphide generated when excreta breaks down non-aerobically.

The severe and significant drawback of any biocide approach is that you may only dump so-treated sewage into city-type sewage treatment plants. Because of this, caravan parks and other waste disposal facilities in rural areas are increasingly and rightly concerned about RV owners' sewerage disposal.

It is essential not to use any product containing formaldehyde as that can wreck an otherwise well-working septic tank.

Napisan

While many specialised chemicals are available, 'Napisan' and Napisan look-alikes are cheap and very effective. Many RV owners use them. All contain sodium percarbonate that breaks down to soda ash and hydrogen peroxide.

Ian Jenkins (now retired Professor of Chemistry and now Professor Emeritus at Griffith University) kindly wrote a definitive article re the use of Napisan for RV toilets for rv-books.com.au.

The professor states 'In my opinion, sodium percarbonate is probably the cheapest, safest, and most efficient product to use in portable toilets, provide you use it as directed'.

Full details (including Professor Jenkins paper and authoritative academic opinion) is at rvbooks.com.au (https://rvb.chaos-central.com/safe-toilet-chemicals-2/).

Other forms of RV toilets

The most commonly used alternative, fitted as standard in most up-market RVs, is similar to the vacuum operated units used in passenger-carrying aircraft.

With these, the contents are sucked down from a stored-vacuum vessel and macerating vacuum pump and then pumped to a large holding tank. Doing so this way enables the toilet and waste holding tank to be positioned apart and located virtually anywhere in the RV.

Another type uses a macerating flush. It's a sort of on-line blender that breaks the waste into a viscous slurry before pumping it into a holding tank.

Composting toilets

An alternative form of a toilet, used mainly in US RVs, composts the waste. This type is more environmentally friendly and, if adequately functioning, does not smell. These toilets do not use water, so no plumbing is required. They are a mini-ecosystem that converts the excreta content into humus, an organic component of soil that takes several months to a year to break down. Excess liquid drains to a separate absorption chamber and then is treated as greywater.

These toilets are used in some of the larger RVs, but mainly by environmentalists as they are bulky and need far more attention than most. There are also strict council regulations regarding disposing of the treated humus as it still contains dangerous content and cannot be used as manure.

Incinerating toilets

Incinerating toilets date back to 1800. They were replaced by water-based sewerage evolved, but are in use once again. Most resemble traditional units but do not need water because they incinerate non-liquid waste products. As long as properly maintained, their only residue is powdery, sterile ash. They are also almost odourless.

A minor downside is that incineration destroys any nutrient content so that residue is not usable as fertiliser. So far, there is no restriction on using incinerating toilets in RVs.

Figure 3.6: The aptly-named Cinderella toilet.
Pic: Cinderella (Norway).

The best known is the Norwegian-developed and made Cinderella (Figure 3.6), that burns the waste there and then. The only residue is ash.

For information on the Cinderella, see: www.retrolooms.-com.au/eco-friendly-incineration-toilets

Another maker is ecojohn products: shop.ecojohn.com/prod-ucts/tinyjohn-waterless-incinerating-toilet

See also inspectapedia.com/septic/Incinerating_Toi-let_Guide.php

Blackwater and dump points

Blackwater is toilet waste (both solid and liquid) and is usually collected in a separate toilet cassette. Dump points are available at most caravan parks and in some 'RV-friendly' towns.

You must not empty cassettes in public or caravan park toilets, but only into authorised dump points provided by some local councils and virtually all caravan parks.

A toilet waste dump point, known formally, as a Sanitary Dump Station) is a properly designed facility intended to receive the discharge of wastewater from any holding tank or similar device installed in any recreational vehicle (RV).

That RV must have an acceptable way of discharging the contents in an approved wastewater disposal system.

Dump points often have a nearby sign similar to that of Figure 4.6.

Figure 4.6: An RAC dump point sign.
Pic: RAC.

Never drain such cassettes in public lavatories and then rinse the container under the publically-used water taps. Such usage can result in exceedingly dangerous contamination because unsuspecting people drink from them. Find out more at www.racq.com.au/Living/Articles/Find-your-nearest-dump-point.

Self-contained RVs

A 'self-contained' RV is one which has a minimal impact on the places it visits. It carries all required water and power (or sustainably generates its power), consumes no local resources and takes all its solid and liquid waste away on departure.

Self-containment is a growing movement in the RV world as concern for the environment grows. It also takes into account the impact of tourists on places of natural beauty and local communities. In some locations including many National Parks, RVs must be self-contained before overnight stays are permitted.

RV laundry and washing machines

Small washing machines are now standard in larger RVs. They can be either top or front loaders (Figure 5.6).

Top-loaders are lighter than a front-loader but use more water. Front-loaders use less water but marginally more energy. They need specialised washing powder if used on their cold cycle.

They can be run from an inverter if mains power is not available. An inverter converts 12 volts dc to 230 or 120 volts ac.

Portable washing machines

Portable washing machines are also available and can be of the single or twin tub variety. You can store one in your tow vehicle or motorhome.

Figure 5.6: This Camec washing machine handles a 4 kg load. It weighs 43.7 kg. Pic: Suncoast Caravan Service.

Clothes washing alternatives

Experienced RV owners say a practical option is to leave the washing (plus water and washing powder) inside a tightly sealed drum in the RV while driving. Or, wash smaller loads by hand.

The mini 'Hills Hoist' is universally popular as a lightweight, folding washing line, but make sure it is secured to the ground with tent pegs on windy days.

CHAPTER 7

Dining and sleeping

In most RVs, the dining area doubles as a sleeping area. While often used, this arrangement can serve one purpose or the other, but not both at the same time. It can also be an issue if one partner is ill or tired, and needs to sleep or rest during the day (but a good case for having an annexe).

The dining area

The dining area in campervans is usually a small table behind the driving cab, with the driver and passenger seats being rotatable when needed. A caravan's dining area is usually larger.

When choosing an RV, give precedence to the sleeping arrangements. The likelihood, or otherwise, of enjoying any RV depends substantially on how well you sleep.

If you sleep well, you can more easily deal with any issues as they arise. If you sleep poorly, those fabulous beaches or sunsets may mean little. Poor sleep also affects concentration, and that is vital when driving.

The primary layout constraint is with the smaller campervans and most camper trailers, their typical lack of width necessitates full-length beds being lengthwise.

Figure 1.7: Many RVs have a dinette that doubles as a bed at night. In this (the author's previously-owned OKA) the table-top drops down to form part of the bed base. Pic: Maarit Rivers (who also designed the OKA's interior).

Types of beds

Island beds have their head ends against an end wall, with space in front and either side. These enable one occupant to visit the loo without disturbing the other. This layout also eases bed-making.

Wall-to-wall beds take up the full width of an RV and are thus located either at its extreme front or rear. These beds take up less space but are awkward to make, and often only accessible from one side. They may require 'partner-hurdling' at night. If the toilet is used routinely during the night, a fore and aft island bed may be preferable to one with no side exits

Drop-down beds usually have an electric mechanism to lower them from the ceiling, generally above an otherwise dining area. These beds save space but lack bedside tables. Make sure that you can access them safely and that their (often space-saving) mattresses are comfortable.

Single beds are an option, even if you use double beds at home, to enable more space between them for access.

RV bed sizes

Most beds in RVs are smaller than those in houses. Take a tape measure with you when you check out an RV and note exact measurements of the bed(s) to make sure whoever sleeps there can fit. Bed extensions are sometimes available, and a few RV makers offer full-length slide-out beds.

Do not be fooled by terms such as 'queen-size'. It is a meaningless marketing term. There are no standard sizes for royalty – let alone their beds.

Bunk beds are an excellent option for young children and can be doubles or triples. Another option is fold-up beds in a fully enclosable annexe, or for teenagers, a nearby tent. Here, the Oztent is a good choice, as it takes only a few seconds to take up and down.

Figure 2.7: End-located bed of the Jayco Al-Terrain caravan. The 'van is also available with the bed sideways. Pic: Jayco.

RV mattresses

When choosing an RV, make sure it is long and wide enough for a good night's sleep. If the supplied mattress is not comfortable (and few are), mattress toppers and insulating mattress covers may help. It's often better to have a new mattress tailor-made.

Avoid the cheap foam mattresses often fitted to new RVs. You might be able to obtain a discount if they are not required.

Airing your bed

Air your bed and bedding regularly. The mattress base must be slatted or perforated to enable condensation to escape but, providing the underneath space is ventilated, extra ventilation should not be needed.

Consider warmth. Layering bed covers can assist as internal temperatures change.

Zippable sleeping bags are comfortable and warm. They take up little space.

CHAPTER 8

RV accessories

There are many seemingly useful or 'must-have' accessories. Some accessories are valuable and should be mandatory. Others, however, may not fit, prove to be incompatible with existing systems, do not work as claimed or never used. These accessories are listed here in an order that is from essential to maybe desirable. (The first two are virtually indispensable).

Keep note of your RVs relevant dimensions, including the need for doors to open and close, and take a tape measure with you when buying.

Smoke alarms

Smoke alarms (Figure 1.8) have been mandatory in all new Australian RVs since 2013. These alarms must comply with Australian Standard AS 3786 and have a push-button that temporarily silences 'false alarms' such as when you burn the toast. They tend to trigger when cooking inside the RV.

As stressed throughout this book, most RV owners do almost all the cooking outside.

Figure 1.8: Kidde RV smoke alarm. Pic: Kidde

If your RV does not have a smoke alarm, fit one now. Their main benefit is that they safeguard you while you are asleep.

Carbon monoxide (CO) detector

Incomplete combustion of, for example, LP gas generates carbon monoxide (CO_2), reducing vitally needed oxygen.

At only 35 parts per million (ppm), carbon monoxide causes headache and dizziness within six to eight hours.

At 200 ppm (about 0.002%), it causes headache and dizziness within two to three hours.

At 800 ppm (0.08 ppm), there is dizziness, nausea and convulsions with 45 minutes, insensibility within two hours and death within three hours.

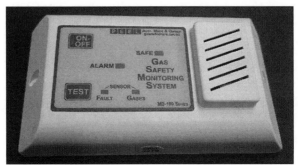

Figure 2.8: Carbon monoxide detector.
Pic: gasdetectors.net.au

If you have LP gas cooking appliances, or LP gas heating inside your RV, a carbon monoxide (CO) detector is potentially lifesaving – Figure 2.8.

Do take this seriously (three caravan occupants died via CO poisoning in Tasmania in 2013).

First aid kit

Many suppliers sell first aid kits of various sizes and multiple needs. These vary from coping with minor cuts, burn and sprains, to those used by paramedics – Figure 3.8. Check that the kit is suitable for coping with first aid essentials in areas that you propose to visit. If towing, ideally have a first aid kit in both vehicles.

Ensure that fellow-travellers know where your kit is stored. If you go bushwalking, take one of these kits, or a smaller, more portable one, with you.

Some medical items have expiry dates. Set up a system that ensures you replace these before they expire.

*Figure 3.8: Always carry a
comprehensive First Aid kit.
Pic: TGA Australia.*

Gain first aid knowledge, e.g. by completing a St. John Am-
bulance course. It will include cardiopulmonary resuscita-
tion (CPR). These courses are offered throughout Australia,
and also via e-learning, DVD or workbook formats, as well
as practical face-to-face training (stjohn.org.au/first-aid-train-
ing).

Also, have a First Aid app:

- www.redcross.org.au/get-involved/learn/first-aid/first-
aid-app

- apps.apple.com/au/app/first-aid-australian-red-
cross/id696880972

- www.androidauthority.com/best-first-aid-apps-android-842599

Tow ball scales

Maintaining correct tow ball weight is critical for trailer stability. Depending on the trailer's weight and length, this may be anything from 75 kg-100 kg for a fully-loaded camper trailer, to the 350 kilograms required by a 3500 kg caravan.

You don't need to take scales with you on every trip. They are virtually essential, however, while experimenting with loading a new trailer correctly.

An alternative is to have a tow ball with a combined 50 mm tow ball with an inbuilt weight gauge (Figure 4.8). The unit shown in Figure 4.8 meets Australia Standard (AS 4177.2 – 2004) for tow balls. This unit is handy also for car carriers, horse floats, bobcats or any changing loads. The scales allow you to instantly reconFigure the trailer or caravan weight to add or subtract tow ball coupling mass.

Figure 4.8: Couplemate tow ball with inbuilt scale. Pic: Couplemate.

See also: rvbooks.com.au/caravan-tow-ball-weight and www.couplemate.com.au/tow-balls/50mm-weigh-safe-tow-ball-scales?

Fifteen amp to ten amp supply cable adaptors

Virtually all Australian caravan parks have only 15 amp supply outlets. RVs consequently have 5 amp supply cables and 15 amp socket inlets.

Appliances typically have 10 amp plugs that fit into a 15 amp socket. A problem, however, is that a 15 amp plug has a larger earth pin than its 10 amp equivalent. This larger pin precludes it from being inserted into a 10 amp socket outlet.

This earth pin incompatibility issue typically arises when seeking to power your RV from your home power supply. The solution to this is an Amfibian adaptor – Figure 5.8.

This adaptor enables you to power an RV when only a 10 amp supply is available. It has a short 10 amp plug and cable plus safety protection (a circuit breaker and Residual Current Device) and accepts a 15 amp supply cable.

Figure 5.8: The Ampfibian unit. The cord (top right) has a 10 amp plug, the centre-located inlet socket accepts a 15 amp supply cable plug. Pic: ampfibian.jpg.

Various types of the Ampfibian are available, for indoor use only, for RVs, or use on construction sites. That for RVs is the (waterproof) Plus unit.

Reversing cameras

Cameras located at the rear of an RV are no substitute (legally or otherwise) for RV reversing mirrors. Cameras cannot see what is down the side of an RV and may also miss overhead hazards such as branches.

As Figure 6.8 shows, reversing cameras do, however, vitally show what may be directly behind the RV.

*Figure 6.8: An RV reversing camera can save lives.
Pic: Nanocam.*

A rear camera needs to be rugged and usable at night. It also needs to be shaded from direct sunlight or it shows only a blank white screen.

Video monitors are available in several shapes and sizes, including dedicated dash and windscreen monitors, and monitors built into a rearview mirror. Check the quality of the monitor image before buying.

To ensure a reliable connection, physical wiring between camera and monitor is preferable to a wireless link.

Spirit level

Many caravan parks, National Parks and free camping areas are surprisingly sloping or bumpy. Spirit levels help you to level your RV in such sites.

Figure 7.8: A two-bubble spirit level like this helps to level your RV fore and aft and sideways. Pic: Source unknown.

There are various types of spirit level: linear and bulls-eye from any number of makers. That shown in Figure 7.8 is the most useful when levelling your RV. It has two linear levels placed at 90 degrees to each other.

For camper-trailers and caravans, attach the spirit level to the top of the A-frame. You can either do this permanently with glue. Or with a rubber band. It is better not to use screws as that requires drilling holes in the caravan's A-frame. Magnetically mounted spirit levels are also available and preferable.

Use the jockey wheel and stabiliser feet to adjust front/rear levels.

For motorhomes, attach the spirit level to a readily viewable part of the vehicle that is to be level, and use short wooden planks as required to do so (see below).

Wheel chocks and levelling wedges

Wheel chocks (stocked by RV accessory suppliers) preclude an RV accidentally moving.

Place chocks in front of, and behind one wheel, on each side once you have positioned your RV.

If your site slopes from left to right, or front to rear, you may need to adjust the RV's tilt by using commercially available levelling wedges – Figure 8.8.

Those wedges made of wood are heavy and deteriorate over time. Plastic blocks are far lighter and usually have gentler inclines. They usefully enable one wheel (or two for dual axle vans) to be driven onto them to increase height on one side.

Figure 8.8: RV levelling ramps. The RV's tyre chock locks into ridges of the levelling device and secures the wheel at the height needed – and safely in place. Pic: Camec.

These blocks are available in various heights and lengths. You need three or more variants. An acceptable alternative is a 'curved wedge' enabling height adjustments of 100 mm or so.

Powered caravan-movers

The ability to manoeuvre a caravan over possibly narrow, curving or sloping urban plots can make the difference between buying and not buying. Dual-axle units are particularly hard to move other than in a straight line.

A powered caravan mover enables you to move a caravan into those tight spots where tow vehicles cannot fit, or to reverse is too challenging.

Caravan movers have various shapes, sizes and van moving capability. Towbar mounted units have rubber wheels or caterpillar tracks to ensure the essential traction – Figure 9.8.

Figure 9.8. The maker states this heavy-duty Camper Trolly Australia unit can move a 4500kg caravan up a 10% gradient: lighter-duty models are available.
Pic: www.campertrolley.com.au

The caravan mover (Figure 10.8) has 12-volt battery-powered motors attached permanently to each side of the chassis. Each drives a roller that can be forced against the tyres, selectively rotating them. The RV's house battery can power some of these units; others have their own.

Figure 10.8: Reich Caravan Mover. Pic: coast-to-coast RVs.

Odds and ends that every RV may need

- Bubble wrap for packing fragile items in cupboards, so they don't break in transit

- Collapsible buckets and bowls to save space.

- Non-skid drawer liners to reduce objects sliding in transit.

- Gaffer and electrical tape to repair just about anything.

- Magnetic hooks (to create extra coat and towel hooks on metal surfaces).

- Pegs for sealing bags and packets as well as hanging out washing.

- Rubber bands for temporary fixing.

- Snap-lock food bags for space-efficient food storage.

- Velcro for fixing fabric, tools, LED lights, and smoke alarms to walls and ceilings.

- Two more items that, as any outback dweller can tell you, are essential. These are:

- A few metres of 12 gauge fencing wire for securing things that move but shouldn't and a can of WD40 for anything that should move but doesn't.

CHAPTER 9
Buying the RV

Having more or less determined your needs, start by looking at RV manufacturers' websites, online brochures and videos. Go to RV Shows and look at display units.

Bear in mind when asking questions that sale staff are hired for that show, have zero RV experience, and may respond with misleading answers. If possible, talk only to the RV makers technical staff.

Seek people who own an RV and ask for their advice. RV owners are usually happy to talk to prospective RV buyers but keep in mind that, unless a complete disaster, their own RV is nearly always the best!

You could even go to a local caravan park and talk to owners there (but ask the park owners first), and read books (particularly this one) and magazines, including those in libraries. See also the many regularly updated articles at rv-books.com.au.

Figure 1.9. Caravan shows can be instructive, but also overwhelming. Pic: caravan and camping show.jpg

Key points to check

When purchasing an RV, the key points to check are mostly in the en-suite area.

Single piece construction is preferable: because it is less prone to water leakage than en-suites with seams.

Figure 2.9: Typical caravan toilet cubicle.
Pic: Australian Motorhomes.

The necessary, slightly-raised shower base reduces the head height. Check that you can still stand upright and can turn without hitting anything.

Water flow through the showerhead and taps needs to be adequate. Checking this is rarely feasible before the RV's completion, so ask the manufacturer about shower flow rates and shower drainage speed. It assists to have more than one drainage point in the shower to ensure drainage when the RV is not level, particularly with a combined shower/toilet.

Make sure the area has adequate lighting (but check it is a 12-volt system) and has fan extraction and grips to ensure you can shower in safety.

From your research, make a list of three or four RVs that you feel are right for you. Compare the cost, comfort, facilities and ease of use of each RV that seems feasible, and see if a preference emerges. If not, keep researching, talking and comparing until you find a clear favourite.

When ready to buy, remember that the RV sales market is competitive, but that not all dealers have staff that have even used an RV – let alone owned one.

Approach a few dealers to discuss buying the RV that you feel is closest to meeting your needs. You are likely to be offered a discount for an immediate buying decision. It is better not to accept the offer unless you are 100% sure that is the RV you genuinely want.

When ready to buy, seek a discount. As sales are fewer than with cars, RV discounts are lower. If no discount is possible, seek free accessories instead.

Try before you buy?

It may seem to make sense to test drive or hire a caravan or motorhome before you buy – but this is not always possible.

Caravans are not straightforward to test drive or hire. A car that hasn't towed before cannot be converted to a tow vehicle in a matter of minutes. It needs a towbar and tow ball, electrical connections, brake controller and towing mirrors.

Caravan dealers rarely allow even adequately equipped vehicles and experienced caravan-towing drivers to test-tow one of their caravans. A few manufacturers and dealers may arrange for a local caravan park to allow a potential customer to stay overnight in one of their own – and tow one there accordingly.

A few hire companies include caravans. If your tow vehicle has the suitable towing equipment, you may be may locate one that has what you seek.

Motorhomes are easier to arrange for a test drive, but you need the appropriate driving licence for any over 4.5 tonnes. Staying casually overnight in a motorhome is also tricky, so it pays to know someone who has one.

Motorhome hire is big business in Australia and particularly in New Zealand. A wide range of hire vehicles is available in both countries.

Be aware that most hire companies cater mainly to those on holiday, not potential buyers. Because of this, vehicles for hire are usually low cost, basic and family-oriented. If you are seeking to persuade a reluctant partner of the delights and comforts of owning a motorhome, hiring may thus not be the best option.

One recent initiative worth considering is peer-to-peer RV hire such as Camplify (www.camplify.com.au) or Share a Camper (support.shareacamper.com/en/support/login).

Both enable private RV owners to hire out their RV when not in use. Both caravans and motorhomes are available for hire under this scheme. RV owners clubs too may be able to help (rvbooks.com.au lists many such clubs).

Buying a used RV

It is generally possible to purchase and then resell a second-hand RV for much the same price. If your budget is limited, buying a used RV makes good sense.

Buying a used RV is also worth considering if you're not sure what type of RV is best for you, or you don't know whether you may like the RV lifestyle. It's also the right choice if you want an RV for a limited period or to undertake only one long journey, such as an 'around Australia'.

When buying a used caravan, keep in mind that they have no odometers (distance counters), so you don't know how far they have travelled, let alone where they have been. On the plus side, however, if they show no sign of dust entry or wet rot, there is little that can go wrong.

Make sure the springs are not sagging, but all that is usually required is renewing brake linings, and replacing wheel bearings and shock absorber rubbers. None is costly, and most are easy to do oneself (if accustomed to working with tools).

Be realistic about what to expect for the van's age, but do not be afraid to ask the seller to correct any minor matters before the sale. If the problem appears significant, look elsewhere.

Be aware that some caravans have inadequate water sealing; this rots the internal timber framework between the caravan's outer skins. Avoid buying any such caravan as such damage is very expensive to repair – and often not feasible.

Be wary of RVs (mostly campervans) that have done multiple rounds of Australia or New Zealand with equally numerous owners.

For your safety and peace of mind, it is vital to conduct a thorough check of a used RV before purchase. Appendix 4 is a detailed 'Used Caravan Checklist'.

The buyer-oriented Caravan Council of Australia (CCA) conducts RV inspections in Victoria primarily for court or tribunal cases. It may occasionally carry out checks for buyers before they take delivery of their new van. The CCA can also usually arrange for this in other states (www.caravan-council.com.au).

Sales contracts, warranties and insurance

Right now (early 2020) the RV industry currently has no standard sales contracts or warranties. RV makers and retailers may thus confuse buyers. They may not state clearly what the RV's warranty covers. For example, is the 'off-road' warranty valid if you drive the RV off-road. Not all warranties are. Or, if they are, how is 'off-road' defined? (See Appendix 5).

If the RV maker or dealer offers a contract and or warranty, it is advisable to have it checked by a lawyer. You need to know and understand what the seller's rights and obligations are as well as your own.

Right now, there are general governmental consumer protection agencies. The only specific body that protects the interests of RV consumers in Australia is the not-for-profit Caravan Council of Australia ('CCA').

The CCA's website includes invaluable advice re what needs including in that contract, (it has a Pro Forma contract that may be of use – or as extra guidance for your lawyer). www.caravancouncil.com.au/rv-buyers.

Important things to know in any RV sales transaction are:

Deposit

How much is the deposit, when is it required and under what circumstances can you recover it? Depending on how you paid it, you may be able to recover the deposit from your financial institution if a dealer or manufacturer goes into receivership after taking your deposit. Talk to your bank or credit card company about this before buying as it is not unknown for dealers and particularly manufacturers to go into receivership to avoid a warranty claim. They often then open again, under a different name, a few days later.

Balance of payment

When is this due and what happens if it is not paid or received in full and on time?

Subsequent Changes

Can you make design or equipment changes to your order before delivery? When is the latest date this can occur?

Cancellations

What happens if you need to cancel your order due to say, ill-health or a change in circumstances?

Delivery

What is the delivery date, and if delayed what happens? What do you need to have installed on the tow vehicle (if applicable) before delivery? Is there to be a full delivery hand-over and how long will this take? Is complete paperwork, such as instruction manuals, supplied?

Checking Tare Mass

If a camper trailer or caravan, ask what will it weigh as delivered to you? Obtain this in writing and file it in a safe place.

Be very careful re this as Tare Mass is usually what the basic unit weighed ex-factory and is currently (2020) not a legal offence if found to be incorrect.

As noted previously, many buyers order 'optional extras'. These are often supplied and fitted by the dealer, and thus not included in that Tare Mass.

If the sales contract includes 'optional extras' insist (in writing) that they are to be included in the declared Tare Mass. If necessary, do this via separate registered letter or email, ticking the box that reveals the sender has opened it.

It is also vital to have the RV weighed on a Certified Weighbridge before making the final payment. In the event of an accident that results in your insurer suggesting overloading may have been a factor that insurance may invalidate your claim. Legally it is up to the driver, not necessarily the owner, to prove that it wasn't. A valid weighbridge docket is often the best form of proof.

Current RV compliance

Currently (early 2020), the responsibility for light trailer compliance rests with its manufacturer, with inspections carried out by some state and territory authorities at the point of first registration. ('Light trailer' includes caravans up to 4.5 tonnes).

Every such Australian RV has a compliance plate fixed to the RV on or near the A-frame in caravans, or door frame in motorhomes.

This plate (Figure 3.9) shows the manufacturer's or importer's name, model name, unique 17-digit vehicle identification number and other crucial information relating to its weight and permitted loads.

There is a certification statement: 'This trailer was manufactured to comply with the Motor Vehicle Standards Act 1989'.

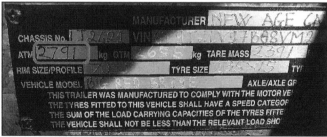

Figure 3.9: Typical (under 4.5 tonne) permanently-fixed Compliance Plate. Pic: New Age Caravans.

Make sure that together with the compliance data, you also receive copies of the following essential documents:

Instruction manuals

These are typically for third-party appliances such as refrigerators, microwaves and TVs. Make sure you have instructions for each device. Many dealers fail to pass them on.

Registration Certificate

New RVs must be registered in the (Australian) state in which they are made. Registration requirements differ by state or jurisdiction (see Appendix 3). If your RV was made in a different state or jurisdiction from where you live, you might need to transfer the registration to your home state or jurisdiction.

Gas and Plumbing Certificate

A gas installation certificate must accompany all RVs that have internal LP gas installations. Items such as slide-out kitchens do not need certifying if you can only use all LP gas appliance externally.

Electrical Safety Standards Certificate

Anyone technically competent can install 12 volt RV systems. A licensed electrician must install 230 volt systems in RVs except in Victoria. That state inexplicably classifies RVs as 'Appliances'. Most local RVs are made in Victoria and may well have been wired by non-electricians.

Buyers should thus include in the purchasing contract a clause to the effect that the maker provides a valid Electrical Standards Certificate. Doing so also eases future resale if sold interstate.

RV warranties

RV warranties vary considerably from one manufacturer to another and from one type of RV to another. Read the warranty covering your RV carefully, as it may contain exclusions of which you need to be aware.

Typical warranty exclusions include 'off-road' use (often with 'off-road' not defined), damage due to immersion in water such as at creek crossings, incorrect loading, incorrect tyre pressures, use of wrong towing equipment and failure to carry out routine maintenance. There are many others.

RV insurance

Insuring your RV for a range of potential incidents is essential. If you are buying your first RV, it pays to take an over-all view of your insurance needs under these new circumstances.

It is not just a matter of arranging new RV insurance alone. RV insurance policies usually only cover lower-cost contents while inside your RV. Existing insurance policies may need reviewing - including home and contents, tow vehicle (if relevant), roadside assistance and medical.

Check too that your 'Home and Contents' policy covers valuable items that you may take with you. Expensive items such as laptops and cameras that you take on your travels are more effectively covered this way. These items are generally covered anywhere out of the home under such policies.

Home and Contents policies also need to be checked regarding wording relating to long periods of absence from home in your RV, since this increases the risk of home theft and damage.

Figure 4.9: Caravan accident. Pic Mudgee Guardian.

If your RV is a trailer, confirm that its towing is covered and if any conditions then apply. Also, check any roadside assistance cover to verify that your trailer also is retrieved if that tow vehicle breaks down. Only the higher levels of roadside assistance may cover this. Check if any towed RV weight or length restrictions apply.

If planning to travel extensively, check your private healthcare cover to see if it covers you for an emergency medical evacuation from a remote area. Private planes and helicopters are expensive!

After completing the above, take out an RV insurance policy that takes into account your needs as well as your current coverage (or lack of it) under other plans.

All-new forthcoming RV regime

There have for many years, been concerns that some manufacturers and importers supply RVs and RV components that are non-compliant in many ways. Further, even when non-compliance is detected, current legislations lack appropriate means of enforcement.

This situation is about to change. The all-new Road Vehicles Standards Act 2018 ensures that light trailers (i.e. trailers under 4.5 tonne) must demonstrate that they meet the relevant national standards. That they do is to be recorded via a statement of compliance provided by the manufacturer or importer. This data is entered on a Register of Approved Vehicles (RAV).

There is currently (early 2020) no legally-set date for the new legislation to come into force, but it is not likely to be before the end of 2022.

The process provides a single point of compliance declaration. That RAV listing enables tracking a non-compliant vehicle. It identifies who made it or imported it.

Manufacturers and importers of light trailers, supplying four or more trailers to the market, must be registered on the Road Vehicle Certification System (RVCS).

There is also a requirement that the manufacturers recommend the RV's tyre size, speed rating and load rating.

See Appendix 3 for an overview of the new Act.

You can access the full Act at www.legislation.gov.au/Details/C2019C00.

CHAPTER 10

Using and looking after yourself and your RV

Safety checks

Especially when towing, look for any changes to the setup of your RV at every opportunity. Each journey (particularly on corrugated dirt roads) may loosen nuts, bolts or screws. Stones or gravel fly up and may cause damage. Check before and after each trip as well as during stopovers.

Walk around the whole rig and look for changes and check under the RV to make sure there is nothing loose or hanging off.

Ensure all internal lockers and items are secure and external lockers are closed or locked. Check the tow vehicle too.

Secure all otherwise loose items inside as well as any on roof racks.

Carry some essential spare parts. Whoever services your vehicle can advise.

If you notice anything that you cannot easily have fixed, get it done out at the earliest opportunity.

Test your brake controller after every hitch-up before driving on the open road. If towing a caravan learn how to apply the brake controller manually to dampen trailer sway, and make sure it is adjusted correctly for the trailer's laden weight.

Check the pressure and condition of all tyres regularly. Ensure you have the equipment (i.e. pressure gauge and compressor) able to inflate/deflate and check tyres away from service stations, especially if going off-road.

If the tow vehicle battery powers a compressor, make sure the air hose is long enough to reach all tyres, those of the trailer. As these compressors draw a fair amount including of energy, have the vehicle's engine running while in use.

Hitching and unhitching

Having a pair of gloves and a cleaning/drying cloth is well worthwhile while hitching and unhitching. WD 40 (for water displacement). Silicon spray for lubrication will often assist to loosen a tight tow ball.

For quick access, keep all hitching gear separately in the back of the tow vehicle or the front of the trailer.

Most Australian states and territories require you to remove tow ball hitches when not in use. This requirement is to prevent sharp objects, corners or edges causing personal injury in the event of an accident.

Levelling the rig

Many (even costly) caravan sites are far from level.

Levelling a caravan must be done with care to avoid unwanted trailer movement or trailer wheels falling off chocks – Figure 1.10.

Use a spirit level, but there is no need to get the bubble precisely in its middle. You can use the jockey wheel to adjust front to back height, then lower the corner jacks accordingly.

Figure 1.10: Levelling a caravan. Pic: OziBlockNChock.

Motorhomes too need wheel chocks, especially on sloping sites.

Tent poles

Twist-and-lock tent poles usually work well and are easy to store. Some need lubricating from time to time.

On firm surfaces, rubber vibration pads used for washing machines add friction at the tent poles base. They also reduce mat damage.

Keep in mind that any point of contact between canvas and pole is a potential source of water ingress.

Mats for annexes

Use annex mats only when needed. If you are fortunate enough to have lush grass under your feet, a mat is probably not necessary (and a mat hampers grass growth).

Choose mats which allow dirt to fall through. The green mesh, sold by the major hardware stores, enables any soil to drop through but does not damage the grass.

Clean mats regularly and dry before storage. Rubber bristles are as effective as nylon brushes and dry more quickly.

Doormats should be of rubber and have holes to allow dirt to fall through.

RV windows

Where feasible, sleep with some windows partly open to reduce condensation, even when cold.

Make sure all windows are closed and locked before travel. Monitor any double-glazing seals and hydraulic arms for damage.

Checking energy usage

Form and reinforce a habit of checking your battery bank's state of charge daily. Establish the minimum recommended state of charge for your battery, and make sure it does not routinely fall below that level. Checking this is vital for lead-acid batteries.

The minimum charge level for lithium (LiFePO4s) is, at about 20%, lower than for most batteries. There is no need to first fully-charge them, even if they are unused for a year or more.

Connecting the supply cable

To avoid handling a live power cable, when hooking up to mains power, firstly connect the power cable, and only then switch on the electricity from the point of supply. When disconnecting, firstly switch off at the supply end.

Power cables are usually wet (from condensation) in the morning. Once disconnected, use a cloth to dry before coiling them up. Velcro straps keep cables and hoses coiled.

Never interconnect power cables.

Always keep them fully uncoiled when in use.

Get to know your RV's electrical system and what should be 'on' and 'off' at different times of the day. Generally, when towing a trailer, only the fridge should be 'on'.

Beware of leaving water pumps switched on while towing. They tend to be activated by minor changes in water pressure as the RV goes over bumps.

Especially if not using mains power, both you and your RV should switch over to a personal 'power saving' mode. Only use mains power for essential tasks.

Fridge usage

Store refrigerated food in freezer bags, or use vacuum packs rather than boxes, for additional storage capacity. Having a full small fridge is more energy-efficient than a half-empty large one. Pack items tightly during transit.

Buy food in small amounts regularly rather than large quantities periodically. Keep as much food in a (non-refrigerated) separate area as possible, such as long-life milk, cereals, rice and soups. Bread can be frozen in small packets and defrosted as needed.

What to store where

Only time and experience reveals how best to use your RV's storage. Do not be surprised in your early RV days if you are always moving items around to find the best area.

Dedicated storage systems are available for 4WDs, but they take a fair time to install and remove. They are also relatively heavy, thereby reducing your remaining payload.

By and large, store items as close as possible to where you use them. Store indoor items inside, outdoor items outside. Store tow vehicle-related items in the tow vehicle.

Establish the warmest and coldest places and store temperature-sensitive items (not needing refrigeration) in the coolest.

If possible, load heavy items in the tow vehicle rather than the trailer. For towing stability, that tow vehicle should weigh as close as possible to its legal maximum (its GVM).

Always store heavy items low and centrally, light items high and, in caravans, as little at the extreme rear as possible. Secure all hard and heavy items before travel. Give away or sell anything which you bought but which doesn't fit, or is not suitable for its intended purpose.

As previously stressed, using an RV changes many a newcomer's lifestyle to cooking outside (using a camp oven if baking is required). The RV's oven is thus rarely if ever used for cooking - only for storage. Do not, however, remove it permanently as first-time RV buyers expect to see one.

It is also common for owners to add some form of fold-down or slide-out outside cooktop, plus a folding table for workspace. Do not, however, add an outdoor sink (space is too limited). Use a plastic bucket instead.

Clothes and shoes

Use layers and add or remove as needed. Take clothes that don't need ironing. Many owners stay overnight in a caravan park every few days to use the laundry. Wash clothes more frequently rather than taking many with you.

Wear whatever is comfortable when travelling. Have one set of 'work' clothes if routinely doing dirty jobs. An excellent source of low-cost clothes can be local op shops – particularly for designer-quality jeans.

Don't carry excess footwear. Have one pair of shower sandals and one pair of thongs, one pair of casual shoes that are also comfortable for walking and a couple of more or less smart ones.

See Appendix 4 for checklists.

CHAPTER 11

Useful RV-related books and information

Wikicamps Australia

This app is almost certainly the most popular used by Australian RV owners. Wikicamps Australia provides a wealth of information on over 40,000 caravan parks, camping grounds, dump points, rest areas and general points of interest (as of early 2020). There are extensive lists of features and prices for each site.

The site has a community-supplied database, which provides continuously updated visitor reviews and photographs of many campsites, giving the latest situation at individual sites.

Community provided reviews can be unforgiving.

Camps Australia Wide

Extensive caravan park and campsite information across Australia is brought to you by the publishers of the widely used (and good value for money) Camps Australia Wide books.

The book has many crowd-sourced reviews. There is a wealth of site information gathered by the publishers, including free camping areas and station- stays as well as commercial sites, National Parks and rest areas. Offline maps and photos are available. An optional subscription enables downloading updates.

Camps 10

This yearly book series is the best known of all Australian campsite guides. At (in 2020) A$50 it is far from cheap, but is comprehensive and updated regularly (www.campsaustraliawide.com/camps-9-books).

Our books and websites

RV Books has, since 2002, published a range of RV and solar-related books. The RV books were published (until mid-2018) under our previous business name of Caravan & Motorhome Books. We publish our solar-related books under the name of Solar Books, https://solarbooks.com.au

The current best seller (as of June 2020) is Why Caravans Rollover - and how to prevent it (rvb.chaos-central.com/why-caravans-roll-over). The Caravan Council of Australia says 'It should be compulsory reading for all caravan owners'.

That book is only followed in sales by (now its fourth edition) Caravan and Motorhome Electrics (rvb.chaos-central.com/caravan-motorhome-electrics).

The book was written for RV owners but has long since become a definitive working manual for auto-electricians. It also used as a text-book by TAFE for its auto-electricians course.

The Caravan and Motorhome Book (rvb.chaos-central.com/caravan-motorhome-book) complements How to Choose and Buy an RV. It covers every aspect of RV usage.

Solar That Really Works (rvb.chaos-central.com/solar-that-really-works) explains all aspects of designing, building and installing solar in cabins and RVs.

Solar Success does likewise for property and home systems.

We update all our books at least once a year, and sooner for vital matters.

Our books are now available for a variety of eBook readers as well as in paperback. You can purchase the Kindle version direct from Amazon. Paperback and non-kindle digital versions are available from a variety of booksellers worldwide. Find out more on our websites.

Our two websites rvbooks.com.au and solarbooks.com have been designed to be a resource for anyone with an RV. As well as information about our books there is a library of constantly-updated articles on all aspects of their respective topics.

CHAPTER 12
About the author

Originally trained a (UK) Royal Air Force ground radar engineer, Collyn Rivers spent two years with de Havilland designing power systems for guided missiles. He then became a research engineer at the newly-formed Chaul End Research Test Centre of Vauxhall/Bedford (vauxpedian.uk2sitebuilder.com/vauxhall-chaul-end-enineering-research-test-centre).

From 1959-1961, Collyn and a colleague (Tony Fleming) drove a 1940 Bedford QLR 4WD truck twice the length and breadth of Africa – including two Sahara crossings (youtu.be/PtG6niRiRXk).

Collyn migrated to Australia shortly after, where he initially designed and built scientific equipment for specialised needs.

In 1971 he founded and edited what became the world's largest-circulation monthly electronics publication (Electronics Today International). It had original versions in Australia, the UK, Holland, Germany, Canada, Indonesia and India.

The Australian version of the magazine was named (by Union Radio Presse Internationale) in January 1976 as 'The Best Electronics Magazine in the World'. It is still the only Australian developed magazine to have had successful overseas editions. Several still exist but under different titles.

Later staff compiled its history: you can access it at en.wikipedia.org/wiki/Electronics_Today_International

The Australian group also produced many associated magazines including Sonics, Comdec Business Technology, Australia CB, Business Computing,

en.wikipedia.org/wiki/Your_Computer_(Australian_-magazine). There were many others, some of which had overseas counterparts.

From 1982-1990 he was technical editor of The Bulletin, and also Australian Business.

During this period Collyn was commissioned jointly by the Australian Society of Accountants and the Federal Department of Industry, Technology and Commerce (DITAC). The task was to write a plain-English book 'The CPA's Guide to Information Technology'.

The book assisted accountants, bankers and financiers in understanding the basics of the new-to-them-technology.

A review of this book in The Australian newspaper (1 December 1987) noted that it 'is written in jargon-free literate English – a bonus for those daunted by the language of technology'.

In 1999, Collyn founded two companies: Caravan and Motorhome Books and Successful Solar Books.

Caravan and Motorhome Books was renamed RV Books in 2018. Daniel Weinstein, the designer and producer of these books and the associated websites, now owns the company.

Collyn still writes the books and most of the websites' articles.

RV Books main website is the now totally-updated website rvbooks.com.au. The solar website is solarbooks.com.au

Figure 1.12: Author Collyn Rivers driving one (of his three) previously-owned Haflingers. These extraordinary vehicles were Austrian-made during the 1970s, primarily for Austrian military use. Some also sold to private buyers. Although weighing a mere 700 kg, a Haflinger can carry 750 kg. They are still widely accepted as the most capable off-road vehicle yet made. The rear-mounted 750 cc twin-cylinder engine is one half of a Porsche 356 engine. This one, made for Australian Airborne Forces, was intended to be dropped by parachute. Pic: Maarit Rivers.

APPENDIX I

Terms and definitions

Many RV-related terms and definitions are commonly mis-understood, even within the RV industry.

Furthermore, weight legislation for camper trailers, conventional and fifth wheel caravans (all known legally as 'trailers') is substantially different from weight legislation relating to campervans, motorhomes and coach conversions.

What is often not understood is the legal and actual difference between actual weights and weight ratings.

Actual weight is just that – it's what something weighs.

A weight rating, however, is a weight set by a manufacturer or by government legislation. It's like a speed limit for driving. You cannot vary that rating and should not exceed it.

RV makers, catalogues, RV magazines and most government legislation may refer to 'mass'. This term has a specific meaning (it is the amount of matter in something). Mass and weight can often be seen as identical, but there are exceptions.

Tare Mass (for trailers)

Tare Mass is the declared mass of a completed trailer ex-factory, i.e. before any extras or payload are added. It is the total mass of the trailer when not carrying any load, but ready for service. All fluid reservoirs (if fitted) are filled their nominal capacity except for 10 litres of fuel (e.g., diesel for a heating device) and all standard equipment and any options.

Note that the term 'fluid reservoirs' does not include water tanks and wastewater tanks fitted to trailers. First-time buyers may not understand that a camper trailer's full water tank may be 50-80 kg; that of a caravan may be up to 250 kg (water weighs 1 kg per litre).

Tare mass is thus an actual weight that is noted on a metal plate usually attached to the front of the trailer's A-frame.

The Tare Mass includes the weight of one 9 litre gas bottle – but not its 8.5 kg of LP gas.

For many trailer makers, 'optional extras', such as air conditioning, interior heating, TVs, solar modules and extra batteries, are obtained and fitted by the dealer. Dealers, however, rarely update the declared Tare Mass.

This consequent exclusion from a trailer's Tare Mass definition of water, gas and dealer-fitted accessories, increases the actual weight of the trailer well above its declared Tare Mass.

This extra weight accordingly reduces the trailer's Payload Allowance (see below).

Buyers should have all trailers weighed in their presence in that 'empty but ready for service' form.

Discuss Tare Mass discrepancies with your dealer before final payment. You must use the actual Tare Mass - not the Tare Mass stated on the compliance plate - to calculate your legally allowable payload.

Aggregate Trailer Mass (abbreviation is ATM)

The ATM is a rating. It is the maximum legal laden weight of a free-standing trailer (i.e. when not coupled to the tow vehicle). The manufacturer sets the ATM – basing it on tyre, axle and suspension load ratings and other considerations.

To check whether your trailer is within its ATM, weigh it - with the jockey wheel down and not coupled to the tow vehicle.

Payload - for camper trailers and caravans

For all RVs, their weight allowance for personal effects is known as their payload. For a trailer it is the Aggregate Trailer Mass (ATM) minus the actual Tare Mass. For many caravans that Tare Mass may well be higher than declared.

Due to the current absence of legal minimums for trailer payloads, buyers should specify a desired, but realistic, payload in their purchase contracts.

Tare Mass - for powered RVs

Tare Mass for powered RV's is the weight of the completed vehicle with full water tanks (1 kg per litre), and 10 litres of fuel (about 7 kg). A powered RV's Tare Mass is usually correct.

Payload - for campervans and motorhomes

Payload, or 'Personal Allowance', for campervans and motorhomes is legally set at 60 kilograms for each of the two sleeping berths and 20 kilograms per berth after that. This allowance is for bedding, cooking utensils, food, books and magazines, plus everything else you may wish to include.

Gross Vehicle Mass - for powered vehicles

For powered vehicles, the Gross Vehicle Mass (GVM) is the most it may legally weigh when fully laden. The vehicle's maker sets the GVM. It is whichever is the lowest of the maximum permissible tyre and axle loadings and the base vehicle's specified maximum weight. It is often possible to have it legally increased.

For powered RVs, the GVM is its Tare Mass plus the weight of driver, all passengers and pet/s plus the obligatory Personal Allowance described above.

In the case of a tow vehicle, it is the maximum fully laden weight of the vehicle, its driver and passengers.

The term fully laden includes the trailer's down-force on the tow vehicle's towbar. Also included are extras such as bull bars, roof racks, second spare wheels, spotlights and winches. It also includes anything on the roof rack or carried on the back of the vehicle.

Gross Combination Mass (GCM)

The GCM is a vehicle maker's legally binding rating that determines the maximum permissible combined mass of the laden tow vehicle and trailer. It includes the weight of the driver, passengers, pets, fuel and water, plus all contents.

The GCM must be measured with the tow vehicle and trailer hitched together with the jockey wheel raised.

Almost all vehicle makers quote the GCM, but while keeping within it is legally binding, there is no legal requirement for a vehicle maker to quote it. In such cases, an email to the maker should result in your receiving the rating.

Maximum tow ball loading - for tow vehicle

The connection between a tow vehicle and trailer consists of a tow bar, a tow hitch receiver and a removable tongue that holds the actual tow hitch coupling. That hitch coupling may be a ball, a pin or other form. Each part has a maximum load rating which you must not exceed.

Where there is a difference in the ratings (usually due to items fitted as after-market accessories), the maximum legal towing load is the lowest.

Caravan mass and speed regulations

Current (2020) Australia's national road rules dictate that for vehicles with a Gross Vehicle Mass under 4.5 tonne, the maximum permissible fully laden trailer weight must not exceed one and a half times the unladen weight of the tow vehicle if the trailer is fitted with brakes, or the unladen weight of the tow vehicle if the trailer does not have brakes.

Forthcoming new Road Rules (see Appendix 2) limit maximum laden trailer weight to be the lesser of the amount specified by the vehicle manufacturer, or the capacity of the towbar.

Besides the above is the limit imposed by Gross Combination Mass (defined above).

A list of public weighbridges is on the National Measurement Institute website (www.industry.gov.au/regulations-and-standards/buying-and-selling-goods-and-services-by-weights-and-other-measures/weighbridges-used-for-trade/find-a-public-weighbridge).

APPENDIX 2

Australian RV Road Rules summary

Some progress was made in 1998 to standardise towing regulations across Australia. Despite that, Australia still has varying rules for towing nationwide.

Which RV road rules apply?

All Australian states and territories have road rules which must be followed by all vehicles.

Beyond these, additional road rules exist for 'heavy' and 'light' trailers depending on their weight or the weight of the tow vehicle towing them. This information relates in general to vehicles and light trailers up to 4500 kg.

New South Wales, South Australia, Victoria and Western Australia, have towing rules that cover tow vehicles up to a Gross Vehicle Mass (GVM) of 4500 kg.

The Australian Capital Territory, the Northern Territory, Queensland and South Australia also have rules that cover trailers with an Aggregate Trailer Mass (ATM) of up to 4500 kg.

Tasmania's towing rules are for 'Very Light Trailers' up to 750 kg, and for 'Light Trailers' up to a Gross Trailer Mass ('GTM') of 3500 kg.

You must follow the laws of the state or territory in which your vehicles are registered, and in the state or territory in which you are travelling.

Maximum trailer dimensions

The 'Vehicle Standard Bulletin 1 ('VSB1') provides maximum trailer dimensions. These are:

Maximum trailer width: 2.5 metres.

Maximum trailer height: 4.3 metres.

Maximum combination length: 19 metres.

Roads, bridges and tunnels (but not multi-storey car parks) are now built nationally with these dimensions in mind; also many existing bridges (particularly in Melbourne, Victoria) are much lower.

VSB 1 also contains additional information on maximum trailer overhang and items that project.

For full details, download VSB1 (infrastructure.gov.au/vehicles/vehicle_regulation/bulletin/index.aspx).

Roadworthiness

All states and territories have regulations on the roadworthiness of trailers. The wording differs, but items covered include requirements to comply with Australian Standards and Australian Design Rules. There are also general comments about the tow vehicle, trailer and its equipment being in good condition and working order.

In short, if it's not compliant and roadworthy, it's not legal.

Trailer weight is the compliance category that statistically is most likely to result in infringements when towing a trailer.

If you exceed any maximum weight limit set by the manufacturer of either the tow vehicle or trailer, you are breaking the law. Note that different weight regulations apply to very old tow vehicles and trailers that do not have the manufacturer's recommendations.

In all Australian states and territories, while towing a trailer, none of the following manufacturer-stipulated weight limits may be exceeded.

Weight limits for the tow vehicle:

Gross Vehicle Mass (GVM), Gross Combination Mass (GCM), Maximum Towing Capacity, Maximum Tow Bar Mass, Maximum Tow Ball Mass.

The tow vehicle manufacturer specifies the first three weight limits. The equipment manufacturer (that may or may not be the tow vehicle manufacturer) specifies the last two.

Tow vehicles have additional weight limits such as tyre and axle loadings. These are taken into consideration by the manufacturer when deriving a tow vehicle's GVM and GCM.

Weight limits for the trailer:

For the ATM, GTM and Maximum Coupling Load, the trailer manufacturer specifies the first two weight-limits (ATM and GTM). The tow ball coupling manufacturer specifies the Maximum Coupling Load.

Trailers have additional weight limits such as tyre and axle loadings. These are generally taken into consideration by the trailer manufacturer when deciding a trailer's ATM and or GTM. There is no legal requirement for the trailer's GTM to be included on the compliance plate.

Visit rvbooks.com.au/rv-weight-definitions for weight definitions of all the above.

Tow bars

Tow bars must be of a suitable type and capacity for the trailer being towed and must conform to Australian Standards. These stipulate that information that must be 'clearly and permanently marked' on the tow bar. That information includes maximum rated capacity, part number, the vehicle model(s) for which the tow bar is intended, and the manufacturer's name or trademark.

Some states require that tow bars must not protrude dangerously or have sharp corners when no trailer is connected. All states and territories have general rules about dangerous vehicle protrusions.

RV electrics

In all states and territories, trailers and tow vehicles must have electrical sockets for lighting and brakes that accord with Australian Design Rules.

The rules stipulate (in detail) the types, colours, positions and visibility of lights. These include brake lights, night lights, indicators, hazard lights, number plate light and reflectors (reversing lights are not compulsory for trailers).

Trailers over 2.2 metres wide must have 'side reflectors' in SA.

In the Northern Territory, trailers over 1800 wide or 1600 mm wide and over 4000 mm long must have 'side marker lamps'.

RV couplings

A coupling is a mechanical connection or 'hitch' between tow vehicle and trailer.

Standard coupling wording in most legislation either refers to or restates the text used in Australian Standards. A typical example is that couplings must be 'strong enough to take the weight of a fully-loaded trailer. Couplings should be marked with the manufacturer's name or trademark and rated capacity.

In New South Wales, the coupling must also have a positive locking mechanism which must be able to be released regardless of the angle of the trailer to the towing vehicle.

In Queensland, the required 'quick-release' coupling must be able to be engaged and disengaged without the use of tools. It must be of a positive locking type with provision for a second independent locking device.

Queensland's and Western Australia's legislation also suggest 'typical approved couplings' for different trailer weights: i.e. 50 mm ball couplings for trailers with an ATM up to 2300 kg, heavy-duty 50 mm ball couplings for trailers with an ATM up to 3500 kg and pintle hook couplings for trailers with an ATM up to 4500 kg.

Tasmania and the Northern Territory additionally state: 'Where any part of the coupling or towbar is removable, the bolts, studs, nuts etc., fastening those parts must have a locking device such as a U-clip, split pin, spring washer, or nylon lock nut'.

Trailer brakes

Trailer brake requirements are now mostly standardised (with minor exceptions) across Australia and depend on the weight of the trailer. The needs range from no brakes for the lightest trailers, brakes on some of the wheels for medium weight trailers to brakes on all wheels for heavier trailers. Heavier trailers additionally need breakaway brakes.

For all states and territories, the trailer brake rules are:

For trailers up to 750 kg GTM (and only one axle in Western Australia and the Northern Territory) - no brakes required.

For trailers between 751-2000 kg GTM, the requirement is for braking on both wheels on at least one axle.

For trailers between 2001-4500 kg GTM, the requirement is for braking on all wheels plus an automatic breakaway system (Australian Capital Territory and Victoria). Breakaway brakes only are referred to in this weight category, not brakes on all wheels.

(In the above categories, New South Wales uses the term 'laden weight' rather than GTM).

Further, brakes must be operable from the driver's seating position. So-called 'over-run' or 'over-ride' brakes (where the momentum of the trailer activates the brake) may be used only for trailers that do not exceed 2 tonnes GTM.

Breakaway brakes

Breakaway brakes operate automatically if the trailer becomes detached from the tow vehicle.

The general requirements are in compliance with Australian Design Rule (ADR) 38. These are that: 'breakaway brakes must operate automatically and quickly if the trailer breaks away from the towing vehicle, and to remain in operation for at least 15 minutes after a break-away.'

Victoria and the Australian Capital Territory additionally require that 'breakaway brakes must be able to hold the trailer on a 12% grade'. A warning device is not a requirement for trailers only visiting New South Wales.

New South Wales (in RMS VIB 6) additionally states that 'to register a trailer in New South Wales, a warning device (either visual or audible) must be fitted in the tow vehicle to warn the driver if the trailer battery charge is not adequate to fulfil automatic breakaway requirements'.

Safety chains

If the trailer becomes disconnected from the tow vehicle, safety chains retain a physical connection between the tow vehicle and trailer.

The general Australian requirement is that light trailer safety chains must conform to Australian Standards (VSB 1). They must be of such size such that their minimum breaking load exceeds the ATM of the trailer. Some states and territories stipulate chain dimensions (taken from VSB1).

Trailers up to 2500 kg ATM must have at least one safety chain while those over that weight must have two. If two chains are used, they must cross over each other.

Chain attachments on the trailer's side must be permanent. Anything attachments on the tow vehicle's sides must use shackles able to withstand the load imposed on them. 'Rated' shackles are not legally required, but RV Books recommends their use.

Safety chains must not touch the ground (when attached) and should stop the drawbar from hitting the ground if the trailer becomes detached. The chains must not prevent a breakaway protection device from operating.

Rearview mirrors

All Australian states and territories require that all powered vehicles must have a clear view of the road, and traffic, ahead, behind and to each side of the driver. This requirement applies equally to tow vehicles pulling trailers. The tow vehicle must have mirrors enabling you to see rearwards along the side of your trailer. Every state and territory generally have similar legislation.

As caravans, in particular, are often wider than the tow vehicle, you need extra (or extended) towing mirrors. These mirrors must not be so wide as to be dangerous to other road users.

Australian Design Rules (ADR 1402) state that towing mirrors may project 150 mm beyond the point of the overall width of the vehicle' or the whole width of any trailer it may be drawing. The mirrors may project 230 mm on each side beyond the point of the overall width of the vehicle provided the mirror is capable of collapsing to 150 mm.

It is common sense and safer to remove towing mirrors when not towing.

Weight distributing hitches

Also known as 'load equalisers', weight distribution hitches were developed to, in effect, assist a tow vehicle in withstanding the nose weight of a heavy caravan.

Queensland's legislation states: 'Many towing drivers use a weight-distribution hitch, particularly when towing large caravans. This device transfers some of the load on the tow bar ball to the towing vehicle's front and rear suspension. This maintains the vehicle's ride height and steering control.'

Western Australia states: 'To tow heavy loads some vehicles may need strengthening, and/or special transmission and suspension options. A load-distributing device may also be required.'

The term 'may' in the above means that you can fit a weight distributing device if you feel you need one - but is not legally required.

See rvb.chaos-central.com/wdhs-and-caravaners-forum copy 1/I

Number plates

All Australian states and territories have rules that state that the tow vehicle number plate must not be obscured by towing equipment, (such as tow bars or tow balls) when not towing.

Likewise, all states and territories have rules on the position and visibility of trailer number plates. One must be at the rear of the trailer and be visible from 20 metres night or day and thus illuminated at night.

An associated requirement is that all number plate, including those of trailers, must easily be read by static and mobile road cameras.

New South Wales and Tasmania require the plates be readable within an arc of 45 degrees above or to either side of the vehicle.

The Northern Territory requires at the plates are readable at an angle of 15 degrees from above for vehicles under 4.5-tonne GVM (but still 45 degrees either side and 45 degrees above for vehicles over 4.5-tonne GVM).

In these states or territories, trailer number plates can no longer be partially-obscured by items such as trailer overhangs, spare wheels or jerry cans.

Towing speed limits

Maximum towing speeds for light trailers are the same as for other vehicles (i.e. the posted speed limit) in the Australian Capital Territory, New South Wales, Queensland, South Australia, Tasmania and Victoria.

In Western Australia, the maximum towing speed is 100 km/h.

Tasmania has a maximum speed limit for all vehicles of 100 km/h on sealed roads, and 80 km/h on unsealed roads.

The Northern Territory's four main highways (i.e. the Barkly, Stuart, Victoria and Arnhem Highways) have a general maximum of 110 km/h, but with sections that permit 130 km/h.

When towing a trailer, you must not tow more than one trailer, nor carry passengers in the trailer.

Learner and provisional drivers towing a trailer

In most states and territories learner drivers are not allowed to tow at all, while provisional (P1) drivers may tow a small trailer weighing up to 250 kg unladen.

In the Australian Capital Territory, this weight limit is increased to 750 kg GVM.

In Victoria, learner drivers may not tow, but P1 drivers can tow a trailer for work purposes or purposes related to agriculture.

If an experienced driver accompanies them a 'Driver Under Instruction' plate must be attached to the front and rear of the vehicle.

In Queensland, learners may tow a trailer if accompanied by a licensed driver.

There are no towing restrictions on either learner or provisional drivers in South Australia and the Northern Territory.

Long vehicle rules

A motorhome, or the combined total length of tow vehicle and trailer over 7.5 metres, is classified as a 'Long Vehicle'.

Its usage must abide by the Long Vehicle rules of the state or territory in which you are travelling. The regulations which RV owners need to be most aware of relate to stopping, minimum distances and turning.

Long Vehicles may only stop on road shoulders outside built-up areas. They may only stop in built-up areas for one hour unless signs say otherwise, or unless picking up goods for the entire period.

If you are driving a Long Vehicle travelling behind another 'Long Vehicle' on a single-lane highway that is not in a built-up area, you must stay at least 60 metres behind that vehicle unless overtaking. In New South Wales, the minimum distance rule applies to roads rather than areas that are not built-up, and lack street lights.

In Western Australia and the Northern Territory, the minimum distance is 200 metres.

In Tasmania, the minimum distance is 200 metres in a 'road train area' or 60 metres otherwise.

Nationally, regulators define a road train as a combination, other than a B-double, consisting of a motor vehicle towing at least two trailers. For this definition, a wheeled converter dolly supporting a semitrailer does not count as a trailer.

Be aware that road trains may weigh up to 152 tonnes and be up to 53.5 metres long. They tend to travel at 100 km/h (62 mph), except in NSW & Queensland where the speed limit for any road train is 90 km/h (56 mph).

Turning left and right

When driving a Long Vehicle, you may use two adjacent lanes to turn left or right as long as you display a 'DO NOT OVERTAKE TURNING VEHICLE' sign at the rear of your trailer. Legally, another vehicle may not overtake you while you are turning.

Legal disclaimer

This guide is a summary and is for general information only.

APPENDIX 3

New Road Vehicle Standards Act

The Road Vehicle Standards Act 2018 (RVSA) enables a new set of Road Vehicle Standards Rules. These Rule substantially change what RV manufacturers can make. Because of this, the industry has been allowed time to enable them to comply. This date is to be late 2022 or 2023.

The objects of the Road Vehicle Standards Act

To set nationally consistent performance-based standards that road vehicles must comply with before being provided in Australia.

To provide consumers in Australia with a choice of road vehicles that:

1: Meet safety and environmental expectations of the

2: Use energy conservation technology and anti-theft technology.

3: Can make use of technological advancements.

4: Give effect to Australia's international obligations to harmonise road vehicle standards.

The Act aims to achieve its objects by:

(a) empowering the Minister to determine national road vehicle standards for road vehicles and vehicle components; and

(b) prohibiting the importation into Australia of road vehicles that do not comply with national road vehicle standards (except in limited circumstances); and

(c) establishing a Register of Approved Vehicles, on which road vehicles must be entered before they are introduced onto the Australian market; and

(d) establishing a framework for recalling road vehicles and approved road vehicle components that are unsafe or do not comply with national road vehicle standards.

This Act regulates the importation and provision of road vehicles. It also regulates the provision of certain road vehicle components.

Road vehicles and certain road vehicle components must comply with national road vehicle standards set by the Minister, except in limited circumstances.

Approval is required to import a road vehicle into Australia and, generally, vehicles must be entered on the Register of Approved Vehicles before being provided for the first time in Australia.

If a recall notice is issued to a person about road vehicles or approved road vehicle components, due to concerns about safety or non-compliance with national road vehicle standards, the person must comply with the notice.

To ensure compliance with this Act, the Department has a range of enforcement powers to ensure the most proportionate and effective regulatory response.

This Act regulates the importation and provision of road vehicles. It also regulates the provision of certain road vehicle components. www.legislation.gov.au/Details/F2019L00198 on the Federal Register of Legislation.

To assist understanding the difference between the exposure draft of the Rules and the latest version of the Rules, the department has prepared a document outlining the key changes between the exposure draft of the Rules and the final version of the Rules.www.infrastructure.gov.au/vehicles/rvs/files/Exposure_Draft_to_Rules_comparison.docx.

A document that identifies how the section numbers and titles have changed www.infrastructure.gov.au/vehicles/rvs/files/Renumbering_Comparison.pdf.

The Road Vehicles Standard Act implements the Australian Government's reforms to the regulatory framework. It should improve the safety, the environmental and anti-theft performance of all road vehicles newly provided to the Australian market.

The Rules prescribe matters relating to the regulation of road vehicles and road vehicle components. In essence, they cover the operational aspects of the Road Vehicles Standards Act, including the information to be included on the Register of Approved Vehicles (RAV).

These include:

- The requirements of the two entry paths.
- The type approval pathway and the concessional RAV entry approval pathway, granting approvals for each.
- Granting Registered Automotive Workshop approvals.
- Approving Model Reports.
- Granting Authorised Vehicle Verifier approvals.
- Granting testing facility approvals.
- Entering vehicles on the Specialist and Enthusiast Vehicles Register.
- Granting of approvals to permit the importation of road vehicles into Australia.
- Granting road vehicle component type approvals.
- Detailing powers to vary, suspend or revoke approvals.
- Establishing a new framework for the recall of road vehicles and approved road vehicle components.
- Publication of approvals and their variation, suspension or revocation.

The full commencement of the Act is postponed until a date to be agreed with industry stakeholders. This date was initially 1 July 2021, but industry pressure was such that it is now unlikely to be earlier than late 2022.

APPENDIX 4

Checklist for buying a used RV

This list is adapted (with the Caravan Council of Australia's approval) from its used caravan checklist.

Helpful tools when conducting an inspection include a torch, a damp checking meter, a ladder and a tape measure. If you can, take along someone knowledgeable about caravans.

Pre-qualifying questions

Is your tow vehicle capable of towing this caravan?

Check the caravan's Tare, ATM and tow ball weight against your tow vehicle's specifications. The CCA strongly recommends weighing the unladen caravan on a registered weighbridge. That weight often exceeds the declared Tare Mass (stamped on a plate usually attached to the A-frame and near the tow hitch).

Is its size, style and layout suitable for your needs?

Can you afford it?

If the answer to any of these three questions is no, don't buy. If yes to all, then make a detailed inspection as follows:

General

☐ Note the caravan's manufacturer and caravan's age. What is the ownership history (if known)? Where has the caravan been kept and where has it been (if known)? Does the manufacturer still exist and are spare parts for this caravan still available?

☐ Is all documentation provided? Ask for weighbridge certificate, gas certificate, and electrical certificate. Is there a service history? Are instruction manuals available?

☐ Compare the VIN plate with documentation provided.

☐ Build type: wood, aluminium or fibreglass?

☐ Overall condition: is the condition consistent with age?

☐ Any signs of repairs, scratches, dents, hail damage, bowing, repainting?

☐ Any sealant around windows and ventilation hatches damaged?

☐ Check that windows open and close and are in good condition.

☐ Axle/suspension: check for stone damage, rust, cracks, deformation.

☐ Under the caravan: check water tanks, wiring, and piping and general under-floor condition. Does the caravan look as though it has been off-road? Through sand, water? Has chassis been grounded?

☐ Tyres: do the tyres have good tread? How old are they? Are the correct tyres fitted (refer to the compliance plate)? Is there a spare tyre?

☐ A-Frame: Is the tow hitch in good condition? Is all electrical wiring present and in good condition? Handbrake, chains, jockey wheel present and working?

☐ Roof: If possible and safe, conduct roof inspection checking for damage, leaks, tree/branch damage, solar panel and TV aerial damage.

- [ ] Electrics: check battery condition, charger, lights and all appliances.
- [ ] Gas: check the condition of gas bottles, regulator and piping.

Interior

- [ ] Smell test: is there any smell of dampness or use of chemicals to disguise other odours? A damp meter is handy for this.
- [ ] Insect test: are there any signs of ants or other insects inside the caravan? Ants like damp wood, suggesting a leak.
- [ ] Walls, ceiling and benchtops: check carefully especially around windows and ventilation hatches for dampness, discolouration, bulges, scratches, indents, holes or evidence of repainting or repair.
- [ ] Cupboards: check for daylight between cupboards and walls, loose or missing screws, doors not opening or closing, broken latches.
- [ ] Beds: check for any damage to the bed, storage area or mattress. Check as for mould in the area under the mattress/s.
- [ ] Kitchen: is the hob/grill/oven/microwave/fridge clean and working?
- [ ] En-suite: is en-suite in good condition? Is a toilet/shower/hot water working? Are there any signs of leaking, mould or poor ventilation?
- [ ] Pop tops: check that the roof raises and lowers quickly and easily, that struts are in good condition and the canvas is not damaged or discoloured.
- [ ] Door: does it open and close and lock? How many keys provided?

- ☐ Awning: check that awning opens and closes appropriately and check canvas condition.
- ☐ Area smoke alarm and fire extinguisher fitted?

Be realistic about what to expect for the van's age, but do not be afraid to ask the seller to correct any minor matters before the sale. If the problem appears significant, look elsewhere.

Be aware that some caravans have inadequate water sealing; this rots the internal timber framework between the caravan's outer skins. Avoid buying any such caravan as such damage is very expensive to repair and often not feasible.

APPENDIX 5

Australian Consumer Warranties

The following information is a summary of Warranties and Refunds, A Guide for Consumers and Business published by the Australian Competitor and Consumer Commission (ACC).

There are two types of warranties in Australian sales contracts: statutory and voluntary warranties. These rights are covered by the Trade Practices Act 1974.

Statutory warranties

Consumers' rights, which the Act says automatically form part of every contract between buyer and seller, are called statutory rights.

'If a seller of goods or services does not meet any one of the obligations, it is a breach of contract with the consumer.

'When this happens, consumers are entitled to a remedy from the seller. The type of remedy depends on the circumstances but may include repair or replacement of goods, compensation for loss or damage, a refund, or having an unsatisfactory service performed again.

'Statutory rights have no set time limit. Depending on the price and quality of goods, consumers may be entitled to a remedy after any manufacturers' or extended warranty has expired.

'Key statutory conditions relating to a sales contract include:

'Goods must be of merchantable quality – they must meet a level of quality and performance that would be reasonable to expect, given their price and description. They should also be free from defects that were not obvious at the time of purchase.

'Goods must be fit for their intended purpose – they should be suitable for any particular purpose the buyer made known to the seller.

'The goods must match the description given to the consumer or the sample shown.

'A consumer must receive clear title to the goods – that is, the seller must be entitled to sell the goods'.

Statutory conditions relating to a service contract include

'Any service must be carried out with due care and skill.

'Any materials supplied in connection with the service must be reasonably fit for the purpose for which they are supplied.

'The service and any materials supplied in connection with the service should be reasonably fit for any particular purpose the consumer made known to the seller'.

Voluntary warranties

Although not legally required to, some businesses offer additional promises about their goods and services.

The typical voluntary or extended warranties, provide additional customer protection if problems arise after a sale. They may also entitle consumers to a refund, replacement or repair in the event of a problem.

> 'This kind of promise, if offered, is in addition to consumers' statutory rights: it cannot overrule statutory rights.
>
> 'When such warranties are provided, consumers should understand their terms and conditions (the 'fine print'). These set out what the seller can do if there is a problem and cover whether there restrictions or circumstances that may prevent a claim. Depending on the terms and conditions, these warranties may entitle consumers to a refund, replacement or repair if there is a problem.'

Voluntary warranties usually apply for a set period – typically 12 months. Such warranties form part of the contract between the buyer and the seller. Consumers have the right to take legal action against the seller if the warranty is dishonoured. This action includes any claims about the future availability of service, spare parts and replacement parts.

Some voluntary warranties, which include manufacturers' warranties, do not cover all types of damage or defects. However, problems that are not covered by a voluntary warranty may still breach a statutory warranty or condition. For example, if the fault means the goods are not of merchantable quality, a consumer may still be entitled to a remedy under their statutory rights. These rights also extend to any warranty claims made by manufacturers or importers.

'Sellers do not have to give refunds, credit or exchanges if consumers damage the goods by using them in a way they were not intended to be used.'

Passing on responsibility for a remedy to a manufacturer

RV buyers frequently allege that when seeking to have a defect remedied, the dealer tells the buyer to 'consult the RV's maker'. Here, the Act is clear:

'Because each sale is a contract between the buyer and the seller, consumers are entitled to insist that the seller provides them with a remedy, even if a problem is due to a manufacturer's fault.

'It is a breach of the Act for sellers to mislead consumers about this right – for example, by claiming they can do nothing and that the consumer must contact the manufacturer for a remedy'.

APPENDIX 6

RV loading and storing checklists

Loading and departure checks

- ☐ When loading, either check everything on the list in one go – or tick off things as you go. If not, you may overlook something vital.

- ☐ Load all heavy items as close to the axle/s and low down as possible, but never at the extreme front or rear.

- ☐ Awning rolled up and locked

- ☐ Ball coupling handle locked

- ☐ Breakaway battery checked for charge

- ☐ External door locked

- ☐ Fridge door closed and locked

- ☐ Gas cylinders secured and gas off

- ☐ Grid power lead disconnected and stored

- ☐ Handbrake released

- ☐ Jockey wheel removed or locked for travelling

- ☐ Overrun brakes reversing lock released

- ☐ Power supply cord disconnected and stored

- ☐ Rear vision mirrors

- ☐ Security chains crossed and attached

- ☐ Slide-outs closed and locked

- ☐ Stabilising legs raised

- ☐ Trailer electric brakes working (check by using the manual lever on the controller).

- [ ] Traffic indicators working
- [ ] Trailer plugs attached
- [ ] TV antenna lowered and stored
- [ ] Water tanks filled
- [ ] Weight distributing hitch set up
- [ ] Wheel nuts tight.

Storing an unused RV

Ideally, store your RV undercover. If this is not feasible, ensure there is ample air space. If using a tarp cover place a few wooden battens between any covering material and the RV, otherwise damp and mildew is inevitable.

For camper trailers and pop-top roofs, make sure the canvas is dry.

If possible, air your RV occasionally.

However, if your RV is stored have blocks under the axle/s, so there is no weight on the tyres.

Turn off any LP gas cylinder, and disconnect any grid power cable. Prop the fridge door/s open to allow air to circulate.

If feasible, use the water pump for a minute or two every two or so weeks. Lack of use (once initially used) tends to cause the pump diaphragm to degenerate.

Deep cycle lead-acid batteries need full-time trickle charging. If you cannot do this yourself, a local auto-electrician may do it for you.

Fully charge AGM batteries, and disconnect the positive lead. In temperate climates, they do not need recharging for about 12 months. Do not attempt to trickle-charge them: it not possible to set any charger to the low voltage required.

In this respect, LiFePO4 batteries are less critical. If 50% charged (and isolated as above), these batteries are not damaged. They hold that charge for many years.

Table of Contents

1. Establishing the essentials   1

Selling your home is a financial trap   2

RV accessibility - for those less mobile   3

How many people may travel in your RV?   5

Accommodating more people   5

2. Towed or self-propelled?   6

Camper-trailers and conventional caravans   6

Caravan safety when towed   7

Fifth-wheel caravans   8

Campervans and motorhomes   9

Travelling patterns   10

Easing the buying decision   10

Who buys what - and why?   11

3. RV categories   13

Tent trailers   16

Basic camper-trailers   17

Up-market camper-trailers   17

Pop-top caravans   18

Full height single-axle caravans   18

Full height dual-axle caravans   18

Toy hauliers   19

Off-road caravans   20

Fifth-wheel caravans   21

Fixed roof campervans   21

Pop-top campervans   22

Slide-on unit campervans   22

Utility conversions (utes)   23

Delivery van conversions   24

Low profile campervans and motorhomes   25

High profile campervans and motorhomes   25

A-class motorhomes   26

Coach conversions   27

'Off-road' motorhomes   28

Expedition vehicles   29

Vintage and restored RVs   31

Self-built RVs   32

Online resources for self-builders   34

4. RV awnings and annexes   35

Annexe materials   36

When and how to use an annexe   36

Awning mats   37

5. RV kitchens   38

Kitchen size and location   38

No need for an oven   39

LP gas cookers   40

Diesel-fuelled cooktops   41

Sinks   42

6. RV showers and toilets   43

Portable showers and toilets   43

RV - basic toilet types   44

Toilet chemicals are needed   45

Bio-stimulant toilet chemicals   45

Biciodic toilet chemicals   45

Napisan   46

Other forms of RV toilets   46

Composting toilets   47

Incinerating toilets   47

Blackwater and dump points   48

Self-contained RVs   49

RV laundry and washing machines   50

Portable washing machines   50

Clothes washing alternatives   51

7. Dining and sleeping   52

The dining area   52

Types of beds   53

RV bed sizes   54

RV mattresses   54

Airing your bed   55

8. RV accessories	56
Smoke alarms	56
Carbon monoxide (CO) detector	57
First aid kit	58
Tow ball scales	59
Fifteen amp to ten amp supply cable adaptors	60
Reversing cameras	61
Spirit level	62
Wheel chocks and levelling wedges	63
Powered caravan-movers	64
Odds and ends that every RV may need	66
9. Buying the RV	67
Key points to check	68
Try before you buy?	69
Buying a used RV	70
Sales contracts, warranties and insurance	71
Deposit	72
Balance of payment	72
Subsequent Changes	72
Cancellations	72
Delivery	73
Checking Tare Mass	73
Current RV compliance	73
Instruction manuals	74
Registration Certificate	74
Gas and Plumbing Certificate	74
Electrical Safety Standards Certificate	75
RV warranties	75
RV insurance	75
All-new forthcoming RV regime	76
10. Using your RV	78
Safety checks	78
Hitching and unhitching	79
Levelling the rig	79
Tent poles	80
Mats for annexes	80

RV windows	80
Checking energy usage	80
Connecting the supply cable	81
Fridge usage	81
What to store where	82
Clothes and shoes	83
11. Useful RV-related books and information	84
Wikicamps Australia	84
Camps Australia Wide	84
Camps 10	84
Our books and websites	85
12. About the author	86
Appendix 1. Terms and definitions	89
Tare Mass (for trailers)	89
Aggregate Trailer Mass (abbreviation is ATM)	90
Payload (for camper trailers and caravans)	90
Tare Mass for powered RVs	91
Payload (for campervans and motorhomes)	91
Gross Vehicle Mass (for powered vehicles)	91
Gross Combination Mass (GCM)	92
Maximum tow ball loading (for tow vehicle)	92
Caravan mass and speed regulations	92
Appendix 2. Australian RV Road Rules Summary	94
Which RV road rules apply?	94
Maximum trailer dimensions	94
Roadworthiness	95
Weight limits for the tow vehicle:	95
Tow bars	96
RV electrics	96
RV couplings	97
Trailer brakes	98
Breakaway brakes	98
Safety chains	99

Rearview mirrors	100
Weight distributing hitches	100
Number plates	101
Towing speed limits	101
Learner and provisional drivers towing a trailer	102
Long vehicle rules	102
Turning left and right	103
Appendix 3. Road Vehicle Standards Act of 2018	**104**
The objects of the Road Vehicle Standards Act	104
Appendix 4. Checklist for buying a used caravan	**107**
Pre-qualifying questions	107
General	107
Interior	108
Appendix 5. Australian Consumer Warranties	**110**
Statutory Warranties	110
Statutory conditions relating to a service contract include	111
Voluntary warranties	111
Passing on responsibility for a remedy to a manufacturer	112
Appendix 6. RV loading and storing checklists	**113**
Loading and departure checks	113
Storing an unused RV	114

141

Made in the USA
Las Vegas, NV
14 October 2022

57280235R00081